MOT

ASSOCIATION
OF WRITERS
& WRITING
PROGRAMS
AWARD FOR
CREATIVE
NONFICTION

MOT

A MEMOIR

SARAH EINSTEIN

THE UNIVERSITY

OF GEORGIA PRESS

ATHENS AND

LONDON

"The Nearest Walmart," "These Small Affections," "Mot Sleeps,"
and "Mr. Brooks" originally appeared in substantially different form
in Ninth Letter 6, no. 2 (Fall/Winter 2009–2010) and in The Pushcart
Prize XXXV: The Best of the Small Presses (New York: Pushcart Prize
Fellowships, 2011). "Wilbur" originally appeared in substantially
different form as "Shelter" in The Sun 446 (October 2014).

Paperback edition, 2018
© 2015 by the University of Georgia Press
Athens, Georgia 30602
www.ugapress.org
All rights reserved
Designed by Kaelin Chappell Broaddus
Set in 9.5/13 Quadraat OT Regular by Kaelin Chappell Broaddus

Most University of Georgia Press titles are
available from popular e-book vendors.

Printed digitally

The Library of Congress has cataloged the
hardcover edition of this book as follows:
Einstein, Sarah.
Mot : a memoir / Sarah Einstein.
x, 152 pages ; 23 cm
ISBN 978-0-8203-4821-6 (ebook) — ISBN 978-0-8203-4820-9
(hardcover : alk. paper) 1. Homelessness—United States.
2. Mental illness—United States. 3. Friendship—United States.
I. Title.
HV4505.E444 2015
362.5'92092—dc23
[B]
                                                        2015006145

Paperback ISBN 978-0-8203-5296-1

British Library Cataloging-in-Publication Data available

FOR MY

PARENTS,

WHO TAUGHT

ME HOW

TO LIVE IN

THE WORLD.

CONTENTS

ACKNOWLEDGMENTS

This book, maybe more than most, has been a communal effort. First, I required the support of friends and loved ones to live in the way chronicled here, which was no small thing. Then many, many writing mentors helped shape that lived experience into a coherent narrative. I'm grateful to everyone who had a hand in either the living or the writing, and particularly grateful to those who had a hand in both.

I'd like to thank my ex-husband Scotti and my not-even-a-tiny-bit-ex-stepdaughter Lucy for their support of both my friendship with Mot and my efforts to write this book. My mother for thinking this was a terrible idea and supporting my doing it anyway. My stepfather for being even more certain that it was a terrible idea and nonetheless slipping me trip money when I'd stop by their home on my way to see Mot. My father for saying only once or twice, "I don't know how anyone could have such damned little sense." My cousins Marilyn and Lois Anne for their supportiveness of all my writing projects, including this one. My sister, Haven, and brother, Robert, for cheering me on, and my niece Kelli for being the very first reader of the very first draft.

I want to thank my husband, Dominik, for his unflagging support and his willingness to marry me despite knowing that he will probably show up in the next book.

I'd also like to thank the people who shaped my inexpert prose into a readable memoir. Kevin Oderman, who has been my friend and writing mentor for more than twenty years, is an indelible part of every word I write, but never more so than in this work. He has been a part of every draft, every revision. Any lovely thing in this book probably began with him. Sara Pritchard helped me recognize and develop the narrative threads in the book and showed me where to cut the parts that weren't needed. Every misstep and tangent cut along the way is probably crumpled up on the floor of her office. Dinty W. Moore, who took a shine to the first chapter in a workshop early on, has championed the work when I was ready to put it aside as unsalvageable. Thank you for making me do those rewrites after I mistakenly thought I was finished.

The MFA program at West Virginia University and the PhD program in Creative Writing at Ohio University gave me the time and the funding to write this book, for which I am eternally grateful. They also provided me with workshop colleagues who read and helped improve several chapters, and I'm grateful to everyone who ever suggested a revision or corrected a mistake. I'd like to particularly thank Sarah Beth Childers, Kelly Sundberg, Rebecca Schwab Cuthbert, Elissa Hoffman, Heather Frese Sanchez, and Lori D'Angelo. I'd also like to thank my more savvy and successful writer friends who have mentored me through the work of going from manuscript to book. Thank you, Laura Bogart and Anna March, for helping me through this process.

But of course, the person I would most like to thank is Mot. It was a brave thing to try to be my friend in spite of all the things that made our friendship difficult, and perhaps an even braver thing to do so while knowing that I was also writing a book about it. He once said, "You can write it, but don't make me read it. What kind of kook would want to read a book all about themselves?" I am grateful to him for his friendship and for his permission to write this book.

MOT

THE NEAREST WALMART

Do not believe a thing because many people speak of it.
Do not believe on the faith of the sages of the past.
Do not believe what you yourself have imagined,
persuading yourself that a God inspires you.
—Buddha

The KOA campground in Amarillo, Texas, sits in a surprisingly seedy neighborhood, more urban than I had expected. A very middle-class couple with impossibly wide smiles advertises an adult video and novelty store from a billboard before the final turnoff to the campground. Cattle graze in a pasture along the road. An unsettling mixture of the bucolic and the pornographic. Rusted trucks sit in the driveways of rusted mobile homes.

I'm here to visit Mot, a new and unlikely friend who wanders from place to place dragging a coterie of dead relatives, celebrities, Polish folktale villains, and Old Testament gods along with him in his head. A month ago he left the home I share with my husband Scotti, stepdaughter Lucy, and another homeless man named Mike in Morgantown, West Virginia, headed for Amarillo because cars, he said, can be had more cheaply out west, and he needed a car.

But more than that, although he didn't say it, Mot had needed to move on. By his own report, he hasn't stayed in any one place longer than three months in more than thirty years. Friends have sometimes lasted a place or two, never many. While they are around his voices are quieter, more easily managed. Having someone real to talk with keeps him grounded, he says, and humor helps.

Still, Mot is dubious about trying to stretch our friendship beyond his time in Morgantown. "There are a lot of bad characters over here," he warned me on the phone, "and most of them don't want you around."

I had planned to pitch my tent where he was camping. Because Mot had called it camping, I'd envisioned an uninhabited wilderness beyond the sprawl of Amarillo. I was wrong. During a rare call from the pay phone at the public library, Mot told me he slept behind an abandoned industrial building on a busy thoroughfare. He had few belongings: extra clothes in a small backpack, an old digital camera I'd given him, a few tools, a wooden-handled knife from Dollar Tree. Each morning, he wrapped these things in a tattered black and red wool blanket he'd found in Romania. After hiding the bundle under a pile of rusted scrap metal near the building, he biked into town to spend the day at the library, at Walmart, or scouting around for a car to buy. In the evening, he retrieved the bundle, stashing the bike in its place. He slept on top of the old blanket, with a pillow made of his extra clothes.

I'd scoured the Web to find someplace more acceptable to stay during my visit. I was as unwilling to stay in a hotel while Mot continued to sleep behind the abandoned building as I was to pitch my tent there beside him. The small one-room cabins and large communal bathrooms of the KOA seemed a workable compromise. I'm comfortable with the idea of being bunkmates but not roommates. Neither Mot nor my husband would mistake bunk beds and communal bathrooms as romantic. And my fascination with Mot is not romantic. It's a remnant of my disappointed desire to change the world and my stubborn belief that one person can do so. Mot says that having a friend, someone to talk to, helps, and the romance of being that person has me in its thrall.

A few days before I left Morgantown for Amarillo, Mot bought a complete wreck of a car for $400 from a kid working at an ice-cream store. He broke camp behind the abandoned building and began staying overnight in the parking lots of the four Amarillo Walmarts. He sent me an email with a picture of his ancient sedan, gray except for one bright blue door, with a bent frame that suggested a tragic past.

I pull into the KOA at noon, having promised to arrive by four. I'm a little surprised Mot isn't here waiting. He and I share a social awkwardness:

we are both early to everything. But I'm four hours early, so I'm not worried. I gather fresh clothes and wander over to the showers to wash away the road. I'm charmed listening to a young mother as she tries to wrangle her toddling son through the rigors of washing his hair. I've stumbled into an oasis of civility. I'd expected the campground to be full of half-drunk bikers and bedraggled women yelling at their children. I'm relieved to have been wrong, but I'm also concerned. Mot will most certainly stand out among these vacationing families and senior-citizen sunbirds. I don't want anyone to hurt his feelings, and I begin to fear that these vacationing Middle Americans might. Folks stop and talk to one another, sharing vacation plans, asking about nearby attractions. I hadn't counted on that. I'm not sure how they will take his just-to-the-left-of-things answers.

The cabin is a medium-sized room with a double bed on one wall, bunk beds on the other, and three shelves. It will be closer for the two of us than I'd imagined, but I'm won over by the porch, which is wide and sturdy and has a swing. It looks out over a parking lot, some tent sites, and then a stockyard; it is not a lovely view. But the wind in Amarillo amazes me. It gusts with such strength that I spend a few minutes sitting on the swing, catching the breeze in my shawl and letting it pull me back, then releasing it and swinging forward again.

The afternoon goes by slowly, viscous and sticky inside the cabin, windswept and dusty on the porch. I'm not good at waiting—it invites worry, which I do too well. I call my husband, Scotti, several times to ask if there's been any word. There has not, and by the third call he, too, is starting to sound a little ragged.

"Maybe you should just spend the night and then drive back," Scotti says. I can't tell if he's worried or annoyed. We've been married only a year, together for two, and are still learning how to understand one another.

"I'm sure he'll show up. I'm just afraid something has happened to him. I checked my email, but nothing."

"How did you check your email? You left your computer here."

"On the phone."

"Oh, for God's sake. We don't have that service. That's going to cost a fortune. Give me your email password and I'll check it for you."

Scotti hadn't blinked at the thousand dollars I'd taken from our meager savings to pay for this trip, but he finds the two or three dollars to check my email beyond the pale. Things are often like this between us. We fight over where to put the pots and pans in the kitchen, whether or not to let the dogs sleep in our bed, what to plant in the vegetable garden. On the big things—buying an old farmhouse, in spite of its damaged roof and rotten windowsills, for the beauty of its woodwork and the size of its yard, making sacrifices to do work we find important instead of work that pays well—we always agree. And at first I took this to mean that we'd be perfect together. Now I'm starting to understand that a marriage is mostly made up of little things, and I'm weary of his complaints about what I buy at the grocery store, how I fold the laundry, the three dollars I spend to have a cup of coffee with a friend at a coffeehouse instead of at home alone. And so I don't give Scotti my password. I'm too tired to even think of a way to sidestep the issue.

"I'm sorry, but even though there's nothing in there you shouldn't see, it makes me squeamish to think of giving you—or anyone—my email password."

"Great. You don't trust me."

"That's not it," I say, and it isn't.

In truth, I am the one who is untrustworthy. There are many things in my email I don't want him to see, mostly the conversations I have with other women about the hard time I'm having settling into this marriage and my doubts about being able to make it work. Scotti is suspicious of my friendships, even of my relationship with my mother. He doesn't believe I should say to anyone something I wouldn't say to him, but there's so much that I can't say to him without starting a fight or breaking his heart. I've stopped talking on the phone because he makes no secret of listening in. He corrects me when he thinks I've said something that I shouldn't, tells me it's time to get off the phone when he thinks I've talked too long. He finds last-minute reasons to ask me to cancel lunches with girlfriends or visits to my family. I am on this trip in part because he has encouraged me to come. Scotti is a psychologist who has sacrificed his career and his license to take care of a single patient, a woman named Rita. Letting me visit Mot is a way to silence my concerns about that relationship and a way to let me have the one friendship he doesn't find threatening.

I don't know what a marriage should look like. I've been married before, but only briefly and when I was much younger. Scotti was divorcing his wife of twenty-three years when we met. When we argue, he says, "Look, this is just what it's like to be in a family. You've been single too long. You don't understand how to change your own behavior to make the household a happier place." In the beginning, I believed him unquestioningly. Now, I'm not so sure. And so my email is full of notes from my mother that begin *if you aren't happy* and from friends who say things like *can't let him control you* and *this isn't okay* and *you need to stand up to him*. Conversations I can't let him see, and I know that if he had my password, he would read them all.

I stand on the porch of the cabin, letting that amazing wind tangle my hair as Scotti and I argue awhile longer. I agree not to use the phone to check email again, but I don't agree to come home. Even if Mot doesn't show up, it would be a lovely thing to spend a week alone in this little cabin.

At a quarter till six, I can't sit in the cabin any longer. I ask the guy behind the counter for directions to the nearest Walmart, and he draws a very crude map on a napkin. I know it's a long shot. There are four Walmarts in Amarillo, and I am not sure I can find even the closest one with the directions I've been given. I have no idea what time Mot usually settles in, or if he's even still in town. I tell myself I'm not going to find him. Then I set out anyway.

I see the old gray sedan with the tragic bent look as soon as I swing into the parking lot. I pull up several feet away and get out of my car cautiously. I can see the very top of a man's head, short gray hair spiked with grime, in the driver's side window, but I can't be sure it's Mot. I'm afraid he may have abandoned the car or given it away, and I'm worried about what sort of person I might startle if he has. The man in the car is slumped over something I can't see. I slam my car door, but the person doesn't move. I call Mot's name, a question in it, and get no response. Left with no other choice, I walk over to the car and lean in the open window on the passenger's side.

There's Mot, pissing into an old soda bottle. He doesn't acknowledge me, and I pull my head out of the car and wait for him to finish. He looks terrible, his hair wild and his face streaked with axle grease and mud. His clothes, a secondhand pair of khakis and an old mechanic's shirt with the name *Ernesto* embroidered on it, are filthy, and the shirt is misbuttoned. He rarely looks as old as his sixty-six years, but today he looks that and then some. Dirt exaggerates the lines around his mouth and eyes. A half-pint of

Scotch sits open on the seat beside him. When he finishes, he puts the lid on the soda bottle but does not zip his pants. He stares out the windshield, unmoving, and I can't tell whether he isn't aware of me or is ignoring me.

I have no idea what to do. I have the sick feeling that whatever I do will be the wrong thing, and if it is wrong enough I may send him screaming from the few comforts he has accumulated since he arrived: the car, the tools to work on it, an extra few sets of clothes. But I must do something.

I walk around to the driver's side of the car and open the door. Mot turns his head toward me, looking more over my shoulder than at me, but he doesn't speak. "Hey you," I prod quietly, "aren't you even going to say hello?"

He sits for a moment more before finally saying, "No, I mean, Sarah never showed up so I figure that's that."

"What do you mean, I never showed up? I'm right here. I've been waiting for you at the campground since noon." I realize he doesn't think I'm real. "I said I would be here on Monday by four o'clock, and I was. You just never came to the camp."

At the word Monday, Mot snaps his head around and looks at me, anger animating his face. "Yes, but you see, this is Tuesday. I went to the campground on Monday and Sarah was not there." He spits the words at me and then cackles. He thinks he has outsmarted whichever of his tormentors has conjured this hallucination of me into being.

"It's not Tuesday," I say firmly. "It's Monday, and I am here exactly like I said I would be." Out of the corner of my eye, I notice a police car swing into an empty space a few yards away, watching.

Mot reaches past the bottle of urine and a coil of old aquarium tubing, fumbles through the garbage under the passenger seat, and pulls out a greasy newspaper. "No, it's not. Today is Tuesday. See, I have today's paper right here." He smacks the front page with his paralyzed hand and then waves it in front of me, triumphant. I peer in, finding the date on the masthead.

"No, look, right here. It says today is Monday." I point.

He looks. He looks again. Suddenly, his features seem to right themselves. He runs his hand through his hair, taming it, and then drops the paper onto his lap, hiding what he suddenly realizes is exposed. "Oh," he says, as if seeing me for the first time, "it's you!"

I move away from the car to give him time to get himself together. I turn my back for a few moments, standing between the sedan and the gaze of the policeman, and then Mot is beside me, his arms outstretched. We hug. He pokes me a few times and sniffs the air near my ear as if to make certain I'm real. "Well, then, let's go to the KOA," he says merrily.

The policeman talks into his radio, his eyes meeting mine as Mot and I finish our hellos, our hugs, and our sheepish apologies. It would be best to get out of here before the cop notices the open Scotch bottle on Mot's front seat, and so even though I'd meant to pick up something for our dinner while I was here, I agree.

We pull up in front of Kabin 1. "I gotta shower," Mot says the minute we are parked. He gathers the things he needs from the trunk of his car. For half an hour I wait on the porch swing, rocking back and forth, trying not to decide I have to go home. Maybe Scotti was right. Maybe I should spend the night and then drive back to West Virginia.

In the parking lot, I saw more of Mot's illness than I'd known was there, and it scares me. I think about his warning. *There are a lot of bad characters over here, and most of them don't want you around.* The reasonable thing would be to offer him the use of the cabin for the time it is already rented, and then simply drive away. But although I can't articulate why I'm here, I'm sure it is not to insist that everything be reasonable.

He finally reappears, smiling broadly as if things have gone perfectly so far, and my fear subsides. He looks younger again, his graying hair neat and growing out of the military cut he'd given himself, with the old clippers we keep for trimming the dogs, on the evening before he left Morgantown a month ago. His skin is wrinkled and tanned. Freshly washed and in clean clothes, he looks more like a retired gentleman with a passion for sailing than one who has been living out of doors, homeless, for over thirty years. And although a close look will show that his left hand is curled into itself and that he drags his left leg a bit, he doesn't look frail or old or crazy. He is, in fact, a little handsome.

We talk about not being hungry and decide against wandering off in search of dinner. Instead, we swing. I tell him about the drive, and he reminisces about his own trips down old Route 66. He retrieves the remaining Scotch from the front seat of his car, and I buy a six-pack of beer from the camp store.

We sit outside for a long time, catching up. Night never seems to fall in Amarillo; dusk stretches on well into what I'd have expected to be darkness. A little into the beer, we start reciting poetry for one another. I pull up things memorized during childhood elocution lessons, mostly Emily Dickinson and a little Shakespeare, though not the best of either. Mot's repertoire is more varied. There is Wordsworth, Coleridge, and the inevitable Kipling. We struggle together through "Prufrock," meeting up only as the mermaids are singing each to each. Then Mot begins to recite from a slew of poets I don't know, men who wrote verse about sailing, cattle drives, saloons, and frontiers. He finishes with Robert Service's "The Shooting of Dan McGrew"—a poem I'd scoff at except it leaves him damp-eyed and melancholy.

> Then on a sudden the music changed,
>> so soft that you scarce could hear;
> But you felt that your life had been looted clean
>> of all that it once held dear;
> That someone had stolen the woman you loved;
>> that her love was a devil's lie;
> That your guts were gone, and the best for you
>> was to crawl away and die.
> 'Twas the crowning cry of a heart's despair,
>> and it thrilled you through and through—
> "I guess I'll make it a spread misere,"
>> said Dangerous Dan McGrew.

His voice, always strong and clear, takes on a brogue that isn't his while he recites, and there is something anachronistic in the whole thing. He isn't old enough to have lived through the world of these poems, but he seems to remember it.

Once we have downed the Scotch and most of the beer, I ask him what happened to make him lose a day. Asking about the goings-on in Mot's peculiar universe is always risky—speaking about the *Big Guys Upstairs* can sometimes summon them.

"I don't know. They can just do that. Drop me down into a dark hole so that I can't see or hear anything, and then when I wake up I'm confused and don't know what day it is or anything." His tone says that this should be obvious and that I've asked a silly question.

I'm always a little startled by how matter-of-fact he is about his delusions, how he forgets that I don't have a direct line into what's going on. "Who dropped you into the hole?"

"It was probably *Moloch*, but I don't know. Coulda been the girls. The *Harpies* were all excited that you were on your way. *They* figure *They* can use you to finally turn me into a girl because I like you, and we want to be like the people we find likable, right?" He laughs. "I mean, I don't want to be a girl, but there you have it. *They* think it's a done deal up here." He motions upward with his thumb.

The daedal hand of delusion paints everything that happens to Mot on an epic scale. Over the months of our friendship, I've learned enough about the characters to follow his stories; like reading *The Brothers Karamazov*, most of the trick is keeping the names straight.

"I tried to talk *Kaiser Bill* or *Moloch* into helping me out because *They* don't want to be girls either, and if I'm a girl, then *They*'ll have to be girls, too. But *They* said nope. Said if I'm going to be a stupid Polack, a Jew lover, I'll just have to be a girl, then. I told you, *They* aren't famous for loving Jews, so *They* don't think I should have anything to do with you." He shrugs and smiles at me. "I guess there is no hope. It's a done deal."

I don't know what to say, so I open the last two beers. Music from a neighboring cabin floats by as the wind changes direction, and suddenly Mot is singing to me. Old songs. Cowboy songs, country songs, even church songs. He sings until the beer bottles are empty. I'm afraid someone might come out and complain about the noise, but his voice is sweet and sonorous, and no one does.

THESE SMALL AFFECTIONS

God
and I have become
like two giant fat people living
in a tiny
boat.

We
keep bumping into
each other
and
l a u g h i n g.
—**Hafiz**

Once Mot and I are comfortable with each other again, we fall back into our Morgantown pattern of nonstop chatter and long drives to no place in particular. Easy conversation and a love of empty hours are part of what binds us together. He is the first friend I've had in years with the time to talk to no purpose or take a drive without a destination. We are aimless and free.

Mot and I had only the slimmest chance of becoming friends. We met four months ago as I was finishing up my tenure as the director of Friendship Room, a drop-in center for adults with mental illness. I'd thought this would be the perfect job for me. I'd worked at the local homeless shelter, Bartlett House, for several years in my twenties, carrying on a family tradition. My mother is a social worker in an office that deals with emergency requests and service linkage, and she populated our childhoods with stories of her clients. My siblings and I rarely met them, but we often helped prepare Thanksgiving dinners or Christmas baskets for them, knew their stories, saw how important they were to her. She has been on the board of the homeless and domestic violence shelters in my hometown since I was a teenager, and she was a founding member of the local Homeless Coalition. This was, then, our cause. It was how we compensated for our privilege in a part of Appalachia where poverty is endemic and we were far from poor. Joining in this work was one of the ways I honored my mother.

I also took the job because Rita, to whom Scotti devotes the bulk of his energies, works here as the lead program assistant. She and I met when she enrolled in Compeer, a program I ran earlier that finds friends for adults with mental illness as a way to help them stay integrated into the community. It was through her that Scotti and I met, and it was because of the amazing progress I had seen her make that I admired him as much as I did. As much as I still do.

Crystal meth and crack had changed the shape of homelessness in the fifteen years since I'd last worked at the shelter, though. At Friendship Room, most of the forty or so people I see during a day are homeless junkies coming in to sleep on the couches or use the phone to make a drug connection. These are not the genteel older men who drink or the timid young men and women with schizophrenia of my years at Bartlett House, and I don't know how to deal with the angrier, more violent homeless men and women who spend their days on the couches there watching television, playing cards, or sleeping. Mot generally avoids such places, but he was already breaking with habit in staying at the shelter. Usually, he chooses to live out of doors. But it has been a cold spring, and he says that he has been trying to learn to live inside again because the cold gets into his joints now. So he followed the flow of the residents from the shelter to Friendship Room because he heard that we were serving up a big Easter dinner, and it seemed to him that a man who was living indoors might also be a man who had Easter dinner with friends. And he had made a few friends, mostly among the older men who were perennially down on their luck but not bad guys. Mot stays away from the younger, more aggressive people. Like me, he's a little frightened of them.

Big feasts always bring in the folk who normally stay away from Friendship Room, preferring the small camps along the river or the larger enclaves outside town. On that morning, while I juggled three hams, two pots of vegetables, half a dozen pies, and all the trimmings, a riverbank dweller named Pam plopped down in a seat near the oven and began to hold forth loudly about how we were all a bunch of sluts and crackheads.

"You fucking whore!" She was talking to me but looking down at her own filthy, bare feet. "You just let all the drug dealers come up here and peddle their dope, and you don't care about the rest of us who really have problems." Her voice got louder and louder the longer she went on. "I'm going to the goddamned police to tell them about what you let go on here, what sort of people you have hanging around up here. They'll lock your fat ass up in jail so long you won't have no teeth left by the time you get out!"

I asked her to keep her voice down and then wrestled the largest ham into a too-small electric roaster, washed my hands, and started to walk toward her, intending to sit and talk with her until she calmed down. But paranoia had turned my few minutes at the counter into an insult or maybe a taunt. As I turned toward her, she pulled out a can of Mace and waved it in my face, still shouting.

"You got drug dealers and rapists working here!" This was true. One of my employees was a convicted rapist who had also done time for selling drugs. Except for my job, Friendship Room hired from within its community of participants. The talent pool, then, required me to find the good in some unlikely people. Errol was clean when I hired him, though he didn't stay that way, and he had enough clout in the local drug scene to keep most of the dealing outside Friendship Room. "What sort of place hires rapists and drug dealers to work with the mentally ill?"

I took a step toward her. "Pam, I need you to leave now. You know the rules. You're barred from Friendship Room for thirty days for threatening violence."

"You want me out of here, you're going to have to call the cops!" She leaned in with the can of Mace. "I dare you, bitch, I just dare you."

One of the more difficult participants, a man sitting on a couch watching television, egged her on. "Mace the cunt, she's got no right to tell us what we can and can't say. It's a free country. We got rights!"

Scenes like this didn't happen often there, although in the next few months they would increase in direct proportion to the amount of crystal meth floating around the homeless community. I was slow to react, and the standoff lasted fifteen minutes until the police arrived. And, as often happened, this first incident set off a series of incidents, some as small as a harsh word, one almost tragic.

Not an hour after Pam was arrested, Rita broke under the stress of having seen me threatened. She often struggles with hallucinations and self-injury, and violence of any sort can send her into a dissociative episode. She was carving the hams, piling slices on a tray that had a long, horizontal crack. Ham drippings were leaking all over the counter and her clothes. When I noticed, I got a larger, undamaged platter from the cabinet and handed it to her. Rita's face twisted with pain and anger and she threw the tray full of meat onto the floor, turned, and ran out the door. I was down on my hands and knees, trying to clean up the mess before someone slipped, when Mike, the program assistant who—against every policy and rule—lived in Scotti's and my basement, ran into the room screaming, "Rita's on the fire escape and says she's going to jump! Call Scotti!"

And so I did, and he came, and he sat with Rita on the fire escape until she didn't want to jump anymore. He was gentle and soothing until she was calm and then boisterous and jocular while joining us for dinner. The clients loved him, even the ones who didn't like me at all. He used that goodwill to make them loyal to Rita as well, but he bought that goodwill by agreeing with them that I could be sour, a bit of a bitch. "Wives," he would say to the men, rolling his eyes. "You know how it is."

Mot later told me that he'd left after deciding that Easter dinner wasn't worth all the yelling. I don't have any memory of him being there. Amid all the chaos, we fed ham, rolls, green beans, pie, and cheerfully decorated Easter eggs to seventy-three people. It wasn't a day when I noticed the comings and goings of the quieter people who had stopped by for supper.

The next two weeks were hard. Rita wasn't able to return to work, and in her absence it became clear that the participants had tolerated me only out of loyalty to her. Without her to take my side, they were increasingly angry at my insistence on enforcing rules the former director had not. If I kicked someone out for being drunk, the older men would spend the afternoon arguing with me about it. They began going to the United Way office down the street to complain about things like my refusal to "give a guy a second chance" or "lighten up a little." And although the folk at the United Way were always supportive and patiently explained our policies to the small groups of angry participants who would show up unannounced, it was tiring for all of us. I was, it was becoming clear, a bad fit for this job.

Still, I didn't want to quit. I wanted to stick it out and ameliorate the problems I thought plagued the place: the drugs, the violence, the exploitation of weaker folk by more savvy ones.

And then everything finally fell completely apart. Almost two weeks to the day after the Easter dinner debacle, I was standing in the hall unlocking the door when a man who looked to be about fifty, in dirty pants and a misbuttoned shirt, pushed me into a corner. I recognized him as the older brother of one of our regulars. I'd heard a rumor from the participants that he'd walked away from a placement in a sex offender program in Chicago and was back in town, but I didn't know if it was true. I did know, though, that even the most hardened of the men who came to the room were a little afraid of him. He was the oldest brother of a family known for its combustible mixture of violence, criminality, and mental illness, dangerous both in his own right and because of the number of brothers and cousins who would mess with anyone who messed with him. When he pushed me into the corner, I was frozen as much by the myth of him as by the way he pinned me to the wall.

He muttered something I couldn't understand and held me in place with one large hand in the middle of my chest while he worked the other around my throat. The blood rushed into my ears and my airway closed. The edges of my vision went dark. I could smell liquor and fried food on his breath, and I remember thinking, "Oh, he must have been drunk last night, but he doesn't smell strongly enough of alcohol to kick him out of the room for the day." As if that were the problem.

Once he had a solid hold on my throat, he moved the hand pinning me to the wall to my breasts, pushing at them and muttering "Oh, mama" to himself. The pushes slowly became soft, then not-so-soft, punches. Just when I felt I might faint, he moved the hand from around my neck to reach for his penis, which I only then noticed was dangling from the front of his filthy trousers. It took me a second or so to realize that I was no longer pinned the wall—that I could get away from him. I pushed him out of the way, opened the door to Friendship Room, ran inside, and locked the door behind me. Outside, I heard him shuffle down the fire escape, still whispering "Oh, mama" to himself. I picked up the phone and hit the speed-dial button for the non-emergency number to the police station.

"It's Sarah over at Friendship Room," I said. "I need you to send an officer over as soon as you can."

"Okay," said the dispatcher. She didn't ask why. I called often enough that anymore, they just came. "Someone will be up there in a minute." The station was across the street. It rarely took more than fifteen minutes for an officer to answer my calls, and I had twenty before it was time to open the room for the day. "Well," I thought, "with any luck I can get this over before everyone starts filing in." And I realized that it had come to this: in the wake of one act of violence, my hope for the day was that I could hide it and so avoid other violences.

Defeated, I wrote my resignation letter while waiting for the police. Perhaps the attack scared me more than it should have. In my years at the homeless shelter, I had faced greater threats and shaken them off. Now I seemed to have lost that youthful feeling of invincibility, but it was much more than that. At the shelter, I was friends with the people who lived there. I liked and cared about them. I enjoyed their company. They understood why I was there, and mostly it was to make them dinner and keep the place clean. At Friendship Room, it was my job to enforce rules nobody wanted to follow, and in a day at work, I did very little that made any one person's life better. The participants didn't like me. They didn't have much reason to. I don't know if most of them would have helped me if they'd been there, or if they would have cheered my attacker on like kids watching a schoolyard brawl. I suspected the latter, which was why I couldn't stay. Of course, it would be a while before I could actually leave. Three months, in fact. Three months is a very long time to get up five days a week and go to a place that scares you in order to tend to the needs of people who don't like you.

It took Mot two weeks to get over the chaos of Easter dinner and return, and if Friendship Room hadn't been the only place in town that gave out free coffee without talking about Jesus, I doubt he would ever have come back. We met on the day after I tendered my resignation. He sat down in the chair next to my desk and complimented me on my shoes, shoes I was inordinately proud of because they were, in fact, very good shoes. He talked about his own shoes, which he didn't like, and a pair of boots he had loved but had worn out walking across Albania. It was the best story I'd heard in my time working at Friendship Room. I spent the afternoon listening to him talk about his travels: camping in a bombed-out Italian monastery; the pretty girls in Nice who gave him wine and books written in English; the students in Turkey who had been sure he was someone famous and insisted that he come stay with them for a few days. After that, I couldn't stop listening to him.

Mot's company got me through the first month after my resignation and before my actual leave-taking. I wasn't doing my job well. I had stopped looking for community partners to run programs, wasn't bothering with the craft classes most days, stopped running the self-advocacy group nobody attended anyway, and just let the participants sleep through the hot summer afternoons. The thugs now knew I could be shaken, and they were doing their best to keep me rattled so I wouldn't notice the empty beer cans in the bathroom or the crack vials hidden behind the radiator. It wasn't working; I saw danger even when it wasn't there. It became harder and harder for me to force myself to go to work. Mostly, I sat at my desk and listened to Mot talk about his travels, or I went into the little office next door and did paperwork. The only productive thing I felt I could do was to leave the files in good order for the next person to do my job, and so I focused on that.

I've traveled to Amarillo in part to get away from the difficulties at work and at home for a while and to burn up the vacation time and personal days accumulated over the last year. I know it's strange that the first new friend I've made in many years is a mentally ill, homeless man who is twenty-five years my senior. But Mot is genuinely my friend, and he understands how difficult the days at Friendship Room have become. Scotti tries to be supportive, but he sees my quitting the job as a failure. Thinks I've made too much of the attack and am using it as an excuse. But Mot says no. He says he has heard the way the men and women talk about me when I'm not there, and that I'm right to be afraid. He, too, thinks they would have cheered on my attacker rather than trying to stop him. He says, "Get outta that place, girlie. Even a dope like me can see that if you don't, you're going to get whacked." He treats my fear as genuine, not as self-indulgence. And I need that right now.

On my first morning in Amarillo, Mot takes me to a diner he says has wonderful waffles. This is a surprise, because my being fat bothers Mot much more than it bothers me. But he is also indulgent and takes great pleasure in finding things he can give to me. Once, he spent an afternoon at the library copying the best cartoons from the *New Yorker* for me, putting them into a little book with a cover woven from scraps of paper. He has given me wine, books, chocolate, garlic, and salt from an ancient sea. A long-sleeved shirt so I won't get sunburned. Two different kinds of scissors. One of a two-pack of wooden-handled knives from Dollar Tree. And now he is taking me out for waffles.

He orders for us both and tells the waitress the same story he tells every time he goes into a restaurant. "I had this friend," he says, "whose mother was a waitress. She was a no-nonsense kind of woman. You'd have liked her." He says this to all waitresses, as if all waitresses would like—or are—no-nonsense women. "So, one day this guy came in and ordered coffee. When she asked him how he wanted it, he said, 'I like my coffee like I like my women.' She'd been waitressing long enough to be sick of that old joke, so she looked him straight in the eye and said, 'I'm sorry. We don't serve stupid coffee here,' and walked away." Mot laughs and looks expectantly at the waitress. She, too, walks away.

Mot is awkward but trying to be friendly with store clerks, waitresses, and campground neighbors. I wince every time someone hurries away from him or listens without answering. I'm not embarrassed for him but angered by people who can't be bothered to be polite once they realize he's smiling a little too broadly, talking with too much animation. I rush into the gap, laugh before the joke is finished, in the hope he won't notice, but of course he does.

I want to follow the waitress and say, "Look, lady, that man got up all the nerve he had to be friendly to you because really he thinks you can see into his soul and you hate him because of what's hiding in there." I want to grab her by the shoulders, march her back to the table and make her say, "Oh, I didn't get it right away, but that was very funny." I want to at least leave her a lousy tip. But Mot might be back here after I'm gone, so I don't. Instead, I leave five dollars under my coffee cup and hope she'll remember him and be kind.

Amarillo turns out to be the perfect place for our visit. There is nothing much to do except drive out to Lake Meredith, look around, make plans to camp out one night without ever meaning to actually do it, take pictures, and talk. Most of the time, I give the keys to Mot. Behind the wheel, he is more centered; he takes on a family-man-out-for-a-drive persona, pulls up a part of himself he has imagined but not lived and tries to make it real. Beside him, I'm also someone else, a person with hours to kill and not much that needs to be done. Relaxed. Companionable. Happy.

We don't get out of the car often, only now and then to look more closely at the desert flowers or to walk around the mostly empty marina. He knows the names of everything. He does not like the ever-present yucca, finding its seedpod obscene, but he delights in showing me my first roadrunner and explaining the dangers of camping in the arroyos. He points out cottonwood, soapberry, and sandbar willows. He explains how the white limestone caprock keeps its place as the softer rock beneath erodes. He holds small spiders in his weathered palm and talks about the different kinds of silk they use in spinning their webs. His voice is rich, melodious. Accentless. Occasionally, to turn me in the right direction to see a thing, he takes my hand or puts his arm on my shoulder. These small affections, at first awkward, soon feel natural.

Mot's knowledge is encyclopedic; perfect recall seems to be a part of his illness, a kind of compensation for the tricks his mind plays when he tries to string together all the events of his life into a narrative that makes sense. When he isn't teaching me the landscape, he tells me stories of his past. Most often, he tells the ones about how he came to be a vessel for the Others. Those stories are hard to hear but are key to understanding the eidola that plague him now. The details in them never change; he recites them the same way he recited "The Shooting of Dan McGrew." If I ask him while he's in the midst of one, he can tell me the color of the shirt he was wearing or what smells were in the air. The skeleton of his life is there, intact, but the connective tissue is all delusion, stories his mind tells itself to explain the horrifying truths in his past. It's the why of things that gives him so much trouble.

> I remember when I was five; my mother took me to the movies. She took just me, not any of my brothers or sisters, and she let me pick out the kind of candy I wanted, and then what was really great was she let me hold her hand all through the movie. I was so happy; I thought she finally loved me. But then, after the movie, we went home and she

told me to get into the oven. I mean, I told you, I wasn't supposed to be born. *Moloch* and *Dubja* had told her that I was supposed to be a girl. I can remember while I was in the womb, she taught me all kinds of things, like how to knit, and showed me the pretty dresses she was making for me. But I wasn't a girl, so she had to get rid of me. I mean, if I wasn't a girl, then I wasn't the promised one, so I was a mistake. She told me it wouldn't hurt, and not to be scared, so I wasn't. I remember the way the grill felt against my cheek. She must have turned on the gas, because I don't remember anything else until our house was full of people. Even my dad had come rushing home from work, and Dr. Dash was there taking care of me. It was the first time they took her away to the hospital. She didn't come back for a long time.

He tells me it's okay to cry, that he understands why someone would cry at a story like this. But I don't, at least not then.

My Italian aunt sent me down the stairs because she wanted to get rid of me. She told me to tie my shoes together. I fell all the way down and busted my head. Then I remember a big hand picking me up, and a voice that said, "Whose dirty baby is this?" That's when they decided I could come back, but only if I brought *Jack* with me. I'd be *Jack*'s second chance, but no one asked me if I wanted this Polish Jesus to take over my life. Sure, some kids might think it was a gift. I mean, before that, I couldn't tell time, and then all of a sudden, the next day in school, I could. And Jack was good at everything. He made friends; he could do all the stuff that people thought was me, but really, anything likable, anything smart, was him. So maybe I should have been grateful. But how can you be grateful when you've got this Jesus inside of you, giving away everything you have, letting all these other people come in to use up all your resources? That's what happens, though, if they try to kill you when you're a little kid. *They* crack you open, and that lets them turn the kid into a Jesus, and then every person who wants to be saved can just glom on to that kid and get a free ride.

I believe these stories, the parts about being put in an oven and sent down the stairs as well as the parts about coming back with a Jesus inside and suddenly knowing how to tell time. I don't doubt that the spirits of his dead aunts live in the moles on his body and that the *Harpies* can send him back down the stairs and into a blackout whenever they want. It's the cosmological argument for the *Big Guys Upstairs*: because there is a Mot, there must also be a *Moloch*, a *Jack*, *Dubja*, the *Harpies*, and the *Dead Aunts*—the ones who created him and control him and without whom he would be plain old Tom again, the Tom he started out to be.

I accept this on faith, resisting Scotti's impulse to replace belief with diagnosis, and hope that acceptance will grow into understanding. And because I believe, he can talk to me and we can be friends.

These are the things we do with ourselves: go to Walmart, go to the lake, swim in the campground's pool, and cook a supper of lentils and rice on a camp stove at the cabin. We are eating lentils and rice not for health or to save money but because we can't find any good alternatives. We've looked for, but not found, a decent restaurant near the campground. Amarillo seems to be a city on its way out. Every evening, we consider the Asian restaurants and taco stands near the campground, but they look too seedy to me, too much a part of the falling-apartness of the neighborhood we are in, and I'm afraid to go inside.

Mot doesn't understand this, but he allows it. "I'm not wanted anywhere," he says, "so it doesn't matter. I just go wherever I want."

We have dinner at an obvious tourist trap toward the middle of the week. Mot puts on a clean dress shirt from Goodwill; I wear a flowery skirt and a white peasant blouse. We say that we are going to celebrate, but we don't say what we are celebrating. The Big Texan Steak Ranch is seedy but in a way that seems sad, not dangerous. It's one of those places with its own gift shop that's advertised on billboards fifty miles out in every direction. It has a seventy-two-ounce steak that, if eaten within an hour, is free. Hostesses dressed like cowgirls and a roving string band dart between the tables of out-of-towners. We order reasonably sized steaks and a bottle of good wine. Here, the waitress laughs at the stupid coffee story. It's like being in the car: a part of Mot that never gets to show itself comes out and the *Others* disappear. We have a good time.

Our visit is mostly made up of these small moments of grace when it seems like things might be better than they have been for both of us: that perhaps Mot will be able to have and keep a friend, that maybe I'm not here on a fool's errand. The vision is beguiling, and it takes some work to remember that the ease with which we get along has as much to do with the fact that we have been lifted from our normal routines as anything. But still, we are proud of ourselves. Amarillo is going better than either of us expected.

The string band comes by to ask for requests, and Mot rescues me when I get lost trying to think of something country by asking first for Vivaldi and then, after everyone has laughed, for "The Yellow Rose of Texas." The waitress hands Mot the check when she brings it, and I slip him the money to pay it under the table rather than reaching for it myself. Without missing a beat, he drops the cash uncounted on top of the bill and stands up, reaching for my hand. We twirl once as the string band plays what Mot says is an old George Jones song called "Hell Stays Open All Night Long" and then giggle ourselves out the door.

MOT SLEEPS

For the sake of the Gentle Friend
who sleeps not by night, do the same!
Entrust your heart to Him and sleep not!
—Rumi

The rich steakhouse dinner doesn't sit well, and I'm up and down all night. Careful not to wake Mot, I search in the dark for my left shoe, my jacket. Under the red and black blanket, Mot sleeps on his belly like a baby in a crib—one hand by his face, the other tossed far out to the side. His breathing is soft and shallow; he doesn't snore. He is peaceful. Nothing suggests that he's battling demons or reliving old terrors. But he is. He has warned me that the *Others* launch their real assault against him at night and not to be frightened if he calls out in his sleep or seems to struggle. He has been told that he screams and thrashes around in his sleep. But here in Amarillo, he doesn't fight at all. Instead, he's unnaturally still.

I curl up in my bed and try to imagine Mot's dreams. Watching him fills me with an aching tenderness, a little maternal and dangerously close to love. I'm afraid for him; I tell myself often that Mot has lived this long without me and will get along just fine when I am gone, but it's a lie. *Just fine* isn't how he has gotten along at all. I don't let myself think about how it will be when it's time for me to go. Instead, I watch him sleep and try to imagine the world I know only from what he tells me in the mornings over coffee.

Mot believes that we all share the same dreamscape and that when I appear in his dreams, I am me, acting with volition, and that when I awake I will remember everything that happened. He holds me accountable. This worries and fascinates me. So far, he has told me of only two dreams that include me, and in both I helped him defeat the *Others* in some nocturnal battle for control of the following day. Together, he says, we were able to hold *Them* at bay. I suspect that this is part of the trick—if I'm an ally now, then later, when the illness creates dreams in which I betray him, it will be more hurtful—and so I don't take credit for whatever help he thinks I've given. "That's not me, no matter what *They* say, you know," I argue, but he won't listen. He tells me to read Jung if I won't take his word for it.

When the sun finally rises, I walk to the pool. After a night of lying quietly awake, I crave movement and noise. When I dive into the pool, cold water snaps the tiredness out of my bones; my head clears with the splash of each stroke. At home I won't swim, too vain to expose my pale, middle-aged body. Here, anonymity defeats my vanity. I spend the morning gliding through the water until I'm empty-headed and my muscles are loose and warm. Between sets of laps I rest on a towel laid against the already warm concrete. When I can't swim anymore and my skin is pink and tender, I gather my things and walk back to the cabin.

Mot has laid out a breakfast of coffee and papaya. He hands me a cup as I walk onto the porch. "I think you should put stevia in it," he says. "I picked some up at the health food store yesterday because you should stop using that chemical stuff."

He wrinkles his nose and gestures to the box of Splenda on the picnic table. Mot suggests, but he rarely demands. He doesn't think I should use the sweetener, but he has set it out anyway. "I mean, have you read the studies on this stuff? They say the scientists who develop artificial sweeteners won't use it. Something about the molecules. It's a conspiracy—Big Business just wants to trick you into buying something you don't need."

This sounds delusional, with its conspiracies and paranoia, but several months ago I'd read an article in the *New Yorker* that mentioned researchers who avoided Splenda.

I'm always conflicted when Mot buys some small thing for me. My gratitude is tinged with guilt when he spends any of the small income he gets from Social Security every month on some trinket that I could easily buy myself, or that I don't want. His money is deposited in an account in Vermont, where he was living when he turned sixty-five, and he accesses it with a debit card he hides in the folds of his old wool blanket. This ingenuity, this surprising ability to survive what seems to me an unsurvivable life, is part of what draws me to Mot. And so, although I find stevia bitter, I use it in my coffee for the rest of the trip.

"How did you sleep?" I ask, throwing a pair of shorts and an old denim shirt of Scotti's over my swimsuit. We sit down on the swing, balancing the plate of papaya chunks between us. The fruit, just past ripe, dissolves into sweet juice as soon as I bite down on it. It's delicious, but it makes the stevia in the coffee taste that much more bitter.

"Lousy. Of course." He rolls his eyes. "A lot going on up here. Mostly the Harpies, but also Dubja and Willie. Something's up, but they won't clue me in on what's happening. That's how things go. I'm not supposed to know anything."

Since I've been here, the Harpies have dominated his dreams. A collective made up of all the women he has known, they speak as one and don't seem to have any real power. The men in his mind give orders, make things happen. The women weep and beg.

"They can only manifest as animals on our plane of existence," Mot explained when he first told me about the Harpies. "That's why animals can talk to me, which is pretty scary. I mean, what does an animal have to say that I want to hear?" He also tells me they run a publishing house in the Northeast. I don't ask how the two things could both be true; he'd have to find a way to explain it, and the explanation would become another layer of delusion. But I'm amused, imagining a publishing house run by housecats and shrews.

He sips his coffee and stares out at the cows in the nearby stockyard. "They say you're a soul sister and they're trying to warn you about the bad characters over here," he says, gesturing upward with his thumb. "You know, that's where you'll end up if I outlive you. You'll be one of them. Only don't be like Harpies. They're not nice women. Most of them just want to get laid—that's why they're always trying to turn me into a girl." He sighs. "That's what I like about you. You're not a woman who gets a few drinks in her and says, 'Let's take off all our clothes!' Kooks like that scare me." He laughs and pats me on the knee.

"What I like about you is that you're always telling me what you like about me," I say, offering him the last piece of papaya, "and you make me breakfast." I also like that sex is out of the question. Mot told me when we first met that he has been celibate for thirty years. He once saw a billboard along the highway with naked women bound and burning in a lake of fire with "Fornicators Will Burn for Eternity" emblazoned across the bottom. Fear of damnation, or of continued damnation, has kept him pure for decades. And because sex has been off the table all along, we are able to be friends without having to guard against it. "I'm going to do the dishes then shower. What do you say we drive out to the lake?"

"Can't," he says without explanation. Mornings are like this; his days are ruled by what happened in his dreams. Once in a while he will tell me why we can't or must do a thing; most days I just take him at his word and don't ask. "Let's drive into town instead. There are some things I need to get at Wally World and this little bookstore I found while biking around the city, and there's something I want to show you."

We putter around the cabin. Mot unpacks and then repacks the trunk of his car. I try once again to arrange the month's worth of clothes I've brought for this one-week trip on the one tiny hanging rod and shelf near my bed. It's an impossible task. They end up folded back in my suitcase or draped over the posts of the upper bunk. Mot sleeps on the lower. My dirndl skirts and summer shirts form a curtain that creates the only real privacy Mot has from me. I can imagine what the *Big Guys Upstairs* must think, though, about him sleeping under a canopy of cotton smocks and batik skirts. *They say I gotta be a girl. Done deal.*

It isn't until well after noon that we drive into town. The knot I've been carrying around in my belly since the day I was attacked loosens a little with every hour we waste. The luxury of doing nothing soothes me, and I fall back into the gentle comfort of Mot's company. For the year I have worked at Friendship Room, I've spent my days with people who either are angry with me or plain don't like me and make certain I know it. I understand why, but it does its damage anyway. Mot's fondness for me, the fact that he says he's better for my presence, heartens me.

The bookstore is a charming, cramped place full of first editions and the smell of leather. Mismatched floral armchairs in ones and twos offer customers a place to sit and peruse. We could easily spend a happy day here, bringing books we've read to one another, recalling the comfort we've found in them. Both of us escape loneliness in fiction. But today we are purposeful, looking for a novel that Mot remembers well and talks of often.

"Do you have *Leaf by Nigel*?" he asks the elderly man at the desk by the door. He names an author I don't know but the bookseller does. For a moment, they talk about his other works—novels that smack of Jack London and Herman Melville and don't sound at all like the book Mot remembers.

"I can't find anything," the shop owner tells us, peering at his computer screen. "Are you sure about the title?"

Mot is, and he begins to recount the story of it. "Nigel is an artist who has spent his life painting a single picture, that of a tree. His neighbor, Parish, is a gardener. Somehow, the painter ends up in an institution, where he and Parish work together to make the forest more beautiful." It sounds familiar to me, but I can't place it. "It's about friendship, and how after we are dead all the things we tried to do here we are able to do in the afterlife. Or at least, that's the hope." Mot looks at us expectantly.

"You mean 'Leaf by Niggle,'" the man tells us. "It's a short story by Tolkien. I don't know if I have it, but I might. Let me look."

He gets up to walk toward the Ts, but Mot stops him. "No, that's not it. The one I want is a novel, and it's called *Leaf by Nigel*. I'm sure of it."

I remember the story now. I read it during my junior high school Tolkien phase. But there is a dangerous look on Mot's face. He has talked about this book often, and it's important to him; I don't know how he would take being confronted with hard evidence that it isn't as he remembers. Better, I think, not to find out.

"I'm sure he's right," I say to the shop owner, who is looking at us oddly now. "Thanks for your help, but we'll just keep looking for *Leaf by Nigel*." I try for an expression that says *please don't push this*. "We'll just look around for a while, if that's okay."

"Sure," the man says. "Help yourself. But I'm pretty sure it's a short story in *The Tolkien Reader*. Just wait here a moment while I find it." Obviously, I wasn't able to arrange my face in the right way to make him understand that he should drop it.

As he turns his back on us to find *The Tolkien Reader*, Mot pulls me out of the store by my arm. "Maybe he's right," he says as he leads me quickly toward the car, watching over his shoulder to be sure the shop owner hasn't followed us. "I don't know. I don't care. But let's get outta here. That guy is a nut!"

I know that of the three of us, the bookseller is undoubtedly the sanest. But this week Mot and I are a law unto ourselves, and this outsider is intruding on what we have agreed to believe is true. In the small world of Mot and me, this makes him dangerously crazy, and we run away from him, laughing.

Once we are clear of the bookshop, we drive around looking for a tree Mot wants to show me. It's hot, but Mot refuses to let me run the air conditioner. "It's bad for your mileage," he insists. He drives the way my father does, window down and elbow out, hand dangling down the side of the door. We circle a middle-class neighborhood near the university, going up and down the same four or five roads as if waiting for the tree to appear where it wasn't a moment before. After an hour, I begin to wonder if it's a real tree, or if he has imagined an incarnation of a tree with leaves by Nigel. I'm not sure which I want it to be; there is something lovely about the idea of spending the afternoon looking for a tree that exists only in a book read long ago and misremembered.

While he drives, Mot tells me more about what's going on in his dreams, warning me.

"The Big Guys Upstairs are trying to find a way to use this all to their advantage," he says, and I know that by "this all" he means me. "Watch out, because I don't always know what the program is. The Harpies warn me sometimes, but not all the time."

As we drive past Mazzulo's Pizza for the third time in fifteen minutes, I realize I'm hungry. "Let's get something to eat," I say.

"Can't. Moloch," Mot says, so we keep driving the same streets looking for a tree that may or may not exist.

"The Big Guys Upstairs are the ones who really pull the strings," Mot says. If the Harpies are Mot's Greek chorus, the Big Guys are the gods on Olympus who arbitrarily dictate the path of his days. "Jack," he says—pronouncing it "yok"—"is a likable guy. Sometimes I think he's the one you like, really. I don't know if you've ever really seen me."

I don't know either, so I keep my mouth shut.

"Jack is the one who learned to tell time, played basketball in high school, had friends, and made people laugh. Anything likable, that's not me, that's Jack," Mot says. "Don't get tricked into thinking that's me, because that just means you'll end up being Jack's friend instead of mine.

That's what always happens. Anything good I get, anything nice, they just take it."

Mot means this literally. We aren't stopping for pizza because *Moloch*, who lives in his throat, is acting up and will steal the food from Mot as he swallows it and use it to feed the *Others*. There are days, maybe more than days, when Mot won't eat. He tries to starve *Moloch* out, but it never works. It leaves Mot weak and feeling like yet another battle has been lost.

Finally, Mot turns left where he had been turning right, and in a block or two we come across a yard with an outrageous garden amid the green, watered lawns. Climbing aster grows extravagantly over a pergola on one side, morning glories over an arbor on the other. Between, hollyhocks, dinner-plate dahlias, tiger lilies, and dwarf sunflowers compete for attention in the explosion of color.

"There is tacky yard art in the subtext of that garden," Mot jokes. "It's way over the top. Someone retired and went nuts!" He laughs and gestures out the driver's-side window. Across the street, a catalpa tree blooms with more modest pastel flowers.

"It's lovely," I say, and it is. Next to the garish, ridiculous garden it looks perfect, every bloom exactly as it should be, the subtle shades outshining the lurid colors of the dahlias and lilies. "Worth the drive." As if the drive itself hadn't been the point.

"I knew you'd like it," he says, and we sit looking at it for several minutes. "Better get going, though. Even in your car, the neighbors are bound to start wondering about the two kooks who are just sitting in a car staring at a tree." He starts the engine again and turns the car in a new direction, away from the pizza parlor. "But no dinner out for us tonight. I don't want to feed these *Come-Alongs* anything nice. Rice and lentils again, my dear!" We laugh and find our way back to the highway and then to camp. It feels like coming home.

Later, well into the twilight that lasts as long as a summer afternoon, I walk to a bench well out of earshot of the cabin and call Scotti. He's growing frustrated with how little time I have to talk while I'm on this trip. But he calls when I'm in the car with Mot or when we're walking by the lake, and I'm afraid of what Mot's paranoia will make of the half-heard conversations. Scotti works at understanding. His clinical experience bears out my concerns about letting Mot wonder what is being said on the other end of the phone, and he knows Mot is afraid of him. Scotti is a mountain of a man; on one of our first dates, children passing on their bikes stopped to stare at him, and one of them yelled, "Hey, Hagrid!" He's nearly six and a half feet tall, with shoulder-length black hair and a big, bushy black beard, and kids often see the Harry Potter character in him. To people my age, he looks like Jerry Garcia writ large. Scotti imagines that Mot's fear comes from being made to feel child-sized next to him, and I'm sure that's part of it. But Mot also says he does not like the way I'm bossed around, and he calls Scotti "the Bully." "You gotta get out of there," he has said. "You're not a kid anymore, you know. You shouldn't let anyone else tell you what to do." And it's a relief to hear that somebody else sees this, even if it's someone who sees all sorts of things that aren't really there.

"Hey," Scotti says. "I thought maybe you weren't going to call at all tonight." He sounds hurt.

"I'm sorry. It's been a long day. A long week. Good, but long." I tell him that it's hard to leave the reality Mot and I have agreed to share while I'm here and ground myself in the ordinariness of discussing bills, vet appointments, and whether the milk in the refrigerator is still good. Hard to step outside the epic so that I can take care of the quotidian. I don't tell him that it's good to be away for a while, that I feel more myself than I have since Scotti and I moved in together, and I'm afraid that talking with him will take some of that away. I don't want to share the details of my days in Amarillo because I don't want to hear his critique of the mistakes he thinks I've made or his suggestions for how I might do things better tomorrow.

"Well, while you're on vacation, I'm fighting the computer tech guys tooth and nail over problems with my summer course and am having a hard time taking care of things around the house. Just because you have time off doesn't mean that I do, and you've left me to deal with everything alone while you're off enjoying yourself."

He seems not to remember that lately I've come home from work too exhausted to do much of anything but watch a little TV, make dinner, and go to bed. Or that neither one of us really worries about taking care of things around the house; we are the sort of people who can live with a little disorder. Our house isn't dirty, but it's messy, a distinction we both insist is significant. We aren't slobs, but Scotti is a pack rat and I'm someone who cleans by throwing everything away. Since I can't throw out his clutter, I let the piles collect. But the sheets get washed every Saturday, and the dishes are always done. And usually that's enough for us.

"I'm sorry, sweetheart. I know how hard you work, and I really am grateful that you're taking care of everything at home while I'm on this trip. Let stuff go as much as you can; I'll take care of it when I get back."

I know he won't let things go. He works hardest when his efforts serve as a reproach. It's always this way: he's too busy to help when I'm there but not when I'm away. He'll clean the house from top to bottom while I'm gone, as if to prove that the day-to-day messiness is really all my fault and that on his own he has a better handle on things. It seems to make him feel better that I have said I'll be home soon, though. He doesn't find all of this—being married, arguing over little things, living in someone else's messiness—as difficult as I do. He has spent most of his adult life married; I've been single most of my forty years. Maybe he's right and that's the problem. Maybe I'm not trying hard enough to learn how to be a wife and a stepmother, although I want very badly to be good at both. I have, though, run off to spend a week with a homeless man to escape those demands, and so the argument that I'm not really working at this carries some weight.

We talk for a while about small things: how Lucy is doing at soccer camp, whether the spots on the zucchini plants in the garden mean he's overwatering, and how Rita says things are holding up at Friendship Room while I'm away. I try to stay on the phone as long as he has things to say, but after half an hour I start to feel anxious. I pretend to be worried about Mot, but really I no longer want to listen to Scotti complain about how much more difficult I have made things by being away. Soon I won't be able to hold my tongue about how life is always like this for Lucy and me, how we can't count on him to be at family dinners or soccer games because we never know when he's going to have to spend the evening calming Rita. How he exhausts all of his patience on her and then comes home dark and angry, and we can't help but feel less important to him because of it. This is an argument that isn't worth having anymore. Already, I know that either I will learn to live with this or I won't, but that the pattern won't change.

"I'm sorry, but I need to get back to the cabin. If I'm gone any longer, I'm afraid Mot will make something of it."

"You know, I'm your husband," Scotti says.

"I know. I love you, and I'll call you tomorrow."

"Yeah. I love you, too. But you need to start thinking about me once in a while."

Back at the cabin, Mot has been cleaning the outside of my car, although his is the bigger disaster.

"You really should get the dead bugs off this thing every day; they are terrible for the paint," he says, wiping a large, unfamiliar yellow blob with wings from the hood. He is washing the whole car by hand with a washcloth and a plastic wastebasket full of soapy water. "Here, take a garbage bag and get the trash out of the backseat." He shakes his head and cleans the grille. "This isn't a bad car, but I hate this." He points to the Toyota insignia. "It's a magic symbol, you know. They put them on our cars to weaken us, so they can take over the world." Still, he worries the chrome with the washcloth until it shines.

"I'm tired," I say. "Let's make it an early night." Last night's sleeplessness and the argument with Scotti have worn me out.

"Yeah," says Mot. "You go ahead. I wouldn't feel like a very nice guy if I let you drive around in this filthy car. I mean, we're friends, so we take care of each other, and this car makes it look like nobody is taking care of you." He starts back to work on the chrome.

I watch Mot, who seems to be imagining himself that same family man he inhabits when we are out for a drive, drawing on a faded memory of the families he knew growing up, the ones he admired in part for their being so very different from his own. Mot often tells the story of breaking his arm during a high school basketball game, a bad break that left it hanging at a strange angle. When he got home, his father—angry at the teenage Tom for not being a better athlete—told him to quit whining and go to bed. "Real athletes just shake this sort of thing off and keep playing." It was two days before his father took him to have the bone set. When he tells this story, Mot takes my hand and runs it over his left forearm. There is a pronounced ridge where the bone healed badly. "I was a real disappointment to my dad," he says. "But he wasn't a good father, not even to the ones of us that he loved." Here in Amarillo, he is trying to make the two of us a different sort of family, if only for the week. It's not exactly playing house; Mot isn't casting me in the role of wife. His affection is avuncular, not romantic.

Instead of going to bed, I bring the book I've been reading, *Truth and*

Beauty by Ann Patchett, out to the porch swing. While he finishes washing the car, I read aloud.

"'Because my life had no shape, I was willing to accept whatever happened,'" I read. "'If Tina had turned to me in that scorching U-Haul and said, Let's keep the truck, let's drive through Canada and take the Alcan Highway to Alaska, I probably would have been thrilled.'"

"Girls," Mot says, putting down the rag. "They always say they want to go to Alaska, but then they never do." He smiles at me. "Except maybe you. You're the sort of kook who might just go."

"Yeah, I just might," I say. And for a moment, I don't know if I am on vacation or running away forever. I'm surprised to find this thought comforting instead of scary. "You never know," I say. "You never know."

MR. BROOKS

As I passed through some of Byberry's wards, I was
reminded of the pictures of the Nazi concentration
camps. I entered a building swarming with naked humans
herded like cattle and treated with less concern . . .
—Albert Deutsch, *The Shame of the States*

On Friday morning, Mot wakes believing that his only remaining sibling, a sister named Elizabeth, has died. He knows, he explains, because she's crying so loudly inside his head that he can't hear me when I speak. Until today, she had not been one of the ones weeping in the background. Mot's angry with her sons for not notifying him.

"How would they have found you?" I ask, and though he can't say, he isn't appeased. The impossible is matter of course for him.

But I've learned a trick, and I use it.

"You know, I think you're wrong. I don't think Elizabeth has died. But if she is dead and living Upstairs, then she must now know that you have been telling the truth about Jack and the Others all along. Right?"

The trick is this: Mot knows that much of what he believes is untrue, that logical inconsistencies distinguish the imagined from the real. It's not possible to attack the heart of his delusions, but the details can be changed if I'm clever and can find a glitch in the logic. It's not a cure. The Upstairsniks have full use of his intellect and eventually fix the flaw. Then he will believe the new, more complicated version of the untruth until a new delusion subsumes and alters the entire narrative of his life that his illness spins. The story has not always been about *Moloch* and *Jack*. The cast of characters "Upstairs" has changed several times over the years. Only the real people and what they've done stay the same. It's part of how he can tell one from the other. "If she knows you were telling the truth, surely she's going to stick up for you? She's your sister! Maybe she'll be the one to make the rest of them leave you alone."

This idea appeals to him. He doesn't buy it, but he thinks about it enough that the crying in his head stops for a while. "Yeah, well, if only it were like that," he says in a way that sounds hopeful.

I ask if he has a phone number I could call to ask about her health, but he doesn't. "Forget it," he says dismissively. "Even if I had a number, they wouldn't tell you. They made it clear years ago they don't want a knuckle-head like me hanging around and won't have anything to do with me."

We go out for lunch and to see a movie. Mot is uncharacteristically adamant: he wants to see *Mr. Brooks*. I haven't heard anything about it, but he has seen the preview and insists. All I can tell from the ad is that William Hurt and Kevin Costner are in the cast and that it is some sort of cop film. Not my sort of movie, really, but I'm not the one who needs to quiet the voices in my head, so I agree.

The theater is in a part of Amarillo we didn't know existed, a newer, wealthier part where we discover all the chain restaurants and coffee houses we had thought were missing. We decide to try Whataburger. Like White Castle and Krystal, it turns out to be one of those quirky, regional places you learn to love as a child or not at all. I'm forty-one; Mot is sixty-six. Even the ketchup tastes wrong to us, a little flat and not quite sweet enough. We dissect our burgers instead of eating them, and we build forts out of the heavy, greasy fries. Mostly, we try not to look like vagrants because we need a place to kill the hour and a half before the movie starts.

Mot talks about his family often enough, but its exact makeup is a muddle to me, and he grows defensive if I ask questions while he tells his stories. I know he had four siblings. There was a brother who lived in the Pacific Northwest and seems to have done well until, in middle age, he killed himself. And, of course, the sister he believes has died. Elizabeth is the only one he ever names, so although he says "my brother did this" or "my sister did that," there's no way to know which of them he means. I believe he had two brothers and two sisters, but it may have been three and one. Collectively, Mot refers to the five of them as the *Five Easy Pieces*, and he says that they have been picked off one by one. As of today, he believes that he is the last one standing. Usually I don't ask questions—I wait for him to tell me what he wants me to know—but today it feels possible to talk him out of believing that his sister has died, so I press when I otherwise would not.

"So, why don't you and your sister speak anymore?" To keep it light, I punctuate the question by launching a pickle into the middle of his french-fry fort with the catapult I've built from two straws and an empty cup. We aren't doing a very good job of looking like normal, middle-class people out for lunch. We never do.

"I've told you," he says, and then for five minutes a disjointed explanation spills out of him—a mess of words with no discernible meaning. The trick of tracking the names doesn't work at all. He forgets to use verbs; affirmative statements become negative ones midsentence; only half a word gets said before he's on to the next. Oddly, he doesn't seem to notice. Finally, he looks me in the eye and says, "See, it's like I told you before. Done deal. Never gonna listen, so I can't talk to them."

Unable to follow any of what he has told me, I pose the question in a different way, hoping for an answer I can understand. "So, if I asked your sister why you don't speak, would she tell me the same thing?"

"No," he answers. "She'd probably tell you it was because I molested her when we were kids. That I was the one who ruined her life. That's what she tells everyone."

That's it. That's all he says. No denial. No explanation.

I look at the man who gentled me through my own fears after I was attacked, an incident that seems insignificant compared to what he has just confessed. It isn't that I don't know that lives are complicated or understand the cycle of abuse. I wouldn't hold this grown man responsible for anything that poor, broken child might have done. I know only a handful of stories, and those are so horrible it's hard to hear them. What would it have been like to grow up in that house? Who was there to teach him what not to do, how not to hurt other people in the same ways he was being hurt? But still, I can't put these two halves of him together and come up with a whole.

I excuse myself and walk to the bathroom to splash cold water on my face. It's a white-tiled, fluorescent nightmare. In the mirror, which is a little warped and so stretches and magnifies my reflection, I look older than I really am. There is a ketchup stain on the sleeve of my shirt, and my hair has kinked into a frizzled mess in the Texas heat. I'm dirty. Tired. Bedraggled. It occurs to me that maybe I don't just look crazy. That I'm a middle-aged housewife come to play at homelessness with a man who believes dead gods live in his throat and who molested his sister, and that this may well mean that I *am* crazy.

We'd chosen to sit in the far back corner, so I have the whole length of the restaurant to watch from behind as Mot cleans up the mess I've made of our lunch. He's careful and deliberate. I look for the boy in the old man, but I can't see him at this distance, or maybe from this angle. He has told me that his mother used to try to pinch off his penis when he was little, to make him the girl he was supposed to be, and he acknowledges but won't discuss other sexual abuses. His confession changes the meaning of these stories for me; my understanding of him is more complicated now. I walk slowly. I try to turn him back into the Mot I knew this morning. But it's impossible not to reflect, to look for hints of predation in his stories, to not be afraid of what I might have let into my life. Everything I've believed about him teeters on the fulcrum of his answer to the obvious question.

In the car on the way to the theater, I work up the nerve to ask that question. "Have you ever touched another child?" I can't imagine what I will do if the answer is *yes*.

He looks at me, his gaze clear, not even surprised. "No. I mean, I've always been attracted to younger people. I'm really a kid, never was allowed to develop into a real person like the rest of you, so it makes sense that I'm attracted to kids because that's as far as I ever got in life. But I know there's a line, and I've never crossed it. Just because *They* hit the old erection button and try to use sex to make me be like *Them*, that doesn't mean I have to do it."

I believe him, but I'm shaken, in part by how much delusion there is in his explanation. Can I trust as truth something so entwined with madness? It's a fragile faith. I have to work to hold on to it. But I'm not ready to let my own cowardice be the thing that separates us.

Mr. Brooks turns out to be movie about a serial killer with an imaginary friend who eggs him on. Costner plays the murderer; William Hurt plays Marshall, a character only Brooks can see, who goads an unwilling Brooks into the killings. After the first gruesome scene I tell Mot I want to leave. I say that I don't think I'm up for this kind of movie right now. I don't tell him how brittle my faith in him is, that I'm afraid the movie might shatter it. He points back to the screen and barks, "Watch it!" in a demanding tone I haven't heard before. On screen, Mr. Brooks is driving while Marshall, who sits in the backseat, tries to convince him to murder a young dance instructor.

"This is just like me. This is exactly what it's like." He pauses for a minute and then adds, "Did you notice I said that in Hurt's voice? Sometimes he's one of the ones over here; he wants me to go to Hollywood to make movies and be one of Them." I have no idea what this might mean, and I'm not asking.

On the drive back to the campground, I try to pull myself together, but I can't. Mot chatters excitedly about the ways in which the movie mirrors his own experience, although he makes sure to say "except for all the killing" every few minutes after I tell him he's scaring me. Once again, I feel like the reasonable thing would be to leave, to pretend I'm worn out and want to start the drive back to Morgantown a little early.

Since lunch, I've been acutely aware of how little I really know about Mot. I may never have even met Tom, the person in whose body all of these gods, daemons, and regular Joes reside. I believe Mot knows there are boundaries and doesn't cross them, but I don't know if he speaks for the rest of Them, or if he even knows what the Others have or haven't done. I remember that he once told me, "They don't like Jews. I mean, I can think of at least one Jew who has died because of the bad guys over here." At the time I'd thought it was more delusion or some reference to Kaiser Wilhelm when he was a living, real person. Now I don't know.

But I feel that Mot is genuinely my friend, and I know the ways in which my world is better, less lonely, because of him. I don't want to run away from him in fear, and I worry about what it would mean for him if I did. But what if Mot is just this sweet, naive guy the Others throw up to get what they need from the world, taking him back down again when they feel like it? What if someday Moloch looks me straight in the eye and says, "We warned you"?

For a few hours, the world feels made of spun glass, everything on the verge of shattering.

Mot says he hasn't been diagnosed with a thought disorder. On days when he can call his experience illness, though, he thinks he must suffer from a dissociative disorder. Scotti is a psychologist who specializes in post-traumatic stress disorders and says, knowing Mot and his story, that the diagnosis fits, but of course he doesn't diagnose people he has met only over the dinner table. Mot has been prescribed psychiatric medication three times, though never by a doctor he saw more than once. He remembers that the drugs made it hard to move, leaving him too vulnerable out on the street, and that they didn't help with the frightening thoughts he was having. Given his age, it's likely he was prescribed drugs like Haldol and Thorazine, drugs that were often used as chemical restraints and that seldom got rid of delusions. They also have terrible side effects, some of which don't go away even after the medication is stopped, including seizures, uncontrollable drooling, and constant tongue-thrusting. Mot finds these possibilities less tolerable than living with the *Others*. "You can't outsmart a seizure," he says.

When Mot was in Morgantown, I tried to convince him to see a local psychiatrist, to try the newer antipsychotics that have milder, less permanent side effects, but he refused. As far as he's concerned, he gave meds a chance and they failed. That's that. Done deal.

Mot remembers that his mother was in and out of psychiatric hospitals during his childhood. Given where he grew up, it's likely his mother was treated at the Philadelphia State Hospital at Byberry, although he either doesn't remember or won't say. Byberry was among the worst of the big state institutions. By his timeline, Mot's mother entered the hospital in 1946 and did not return home until 1949. Albert Deutsch wrote *The Shame of the States* in 1948. It's very possible, even probable, that Mot's mother was among his "swarm of naked humans herded like cattle." Patients weren't provided with hospital clothing. They wore whatever they had on when they got to Byberry until it rotted from their bodies, and then they went without. Three years is a lot to expect of a cotton dress or slacks and a sweater—what a mother might have worn in the forties to take her son to the movies.

I understand why he refuses treatment. There are worse lives to have lived than his; his mother's may well have been one such life.

We arrive at the cabin in the late afternoon, surprised at how early it still is; we don't have the strength for a day so long. I swim and Mot naps. The campground has filled with weekend campers. The pool roils with children, wound up by long car rides, and haggard parents, who toss themselves onto the deck chairs and shut their eyes. I wonder if my own fragile trust is enough to make it all right that I've brought Mot among them. I'm glad he is napping rather than swimming with me. I don't want to have to watch him watching the children play or to wonder what he's thinking as he does. My fear is an ugly, alien thing. I don't know how our friendship can survive it.

It's easy to identify the events that break us, harder to name the myriad tiny things that knit us back together. Saturday morning hurries by in a series of necessary tasks. We pack and load the cars so our last hours can be spent on better things. Mot sorts the camping gear and cleans the cabin while I do the laundry. Together, we divide up what we've acquired over the week. He takes the coffee pot, the hotplate, and the leftover rice and lentils. I keep the bottle of stevia, the straw basket, and the wild alfalfa he harvested for a tea we never made. We make our last pilgrimage to Walmart. Mot buys engine additives for my car that I think may do more harm than good but allow anyway. He accepts a prepaid cell phone from me, the kind criminals on cop shows use and then throw away, although he can't go so far as to promise he'll use it.

We drive out to the lake one more time so I can get a picture of the hand-painted "Buffalo Barn Buck-Out—Parking $2—Not Responsible for Accidents" sign. The sun seems to be always in my eyes. No matter which way we turn, there it is, over the horizon. It takes us three passes around the lake to find the right road, because I can only look at things sideways through the glare. When we get out to take pictures, I have to hold the camera blindly in front of me; looking through the viewfinder leaves dark afterimages burned into my field of vision.

"It's a bright one," Mot says, handing me his broken pair of Dollar Tree sunglasses. "You'll need these more than I will, since you're driving." He chucks me on the shoulder.

"You can drive if you like," I offer.

"Maybe I better. The way you're looking today, I don't know, it might be a disaster." Mot shields his eyes with his hand and points to the rusted shell of a VW bus among the yucca. "Probably that guy had the same sort of knucklebrained idea you would have. Just drive your car into the desert and live in it until you're sane again. No, definitely better if I do the driving for now."

I don't say that I would never have that idea and that I don't think the owner of the bus was trying to drive himself sane. Mot thinks we all have ancestors and dead gods to outrun, and I can't see any reason to tell him that he has it worse than most of us. I toss him the keys and the broken sunglasses, crawl into the passenger seat, and flip through the radio stations until I find NPR.

"Ah, Wagner." Mot scoots the driver's seat as far toward the steering wheel as it will go and squeezes himself into the car. "I like Wagner, but we can't listen to him. It will wake up old *Kaiser Willie*. Better turn to something else." He fiddles with the dial a moment, snorting disgustedly at every station he finds, and then turns the radio off. "Sometimes silence is best," he says.

On the trip back to town, I start to cry. I can't explain why, but Mot doesn't ask. He pulls the car to the side of the road, gets out, walks over, and opens my door. He puts an arm over my shoulder and walks me down into one of the arroyos.

"Once," he says, "I decided to camp in one just to see. I mean, if I was supposed to die, it seemed as good a way as any. But there wasn't any rain that night, or the next, and so I figured what the hell and walked into town for a beer."

This is the first story he has told me that I know doesn't have even a grain of truth in it. I call him a liar, and he smiles. I laugh. He chucks me under the chin, like I'm some child who has scraped her knee. "It's gonna be okay," he says, and then he walks back to the car.

We spend our last evening quietly, reading to one another, making a meal of the last of the fruit, bread, and cheese we bought during the week. He gets out the road atlas and marks good stopping places on my route home. I sew missing buttons onto his shirts. Mot's revelation has changed things but not ruined them. There is warmth and comfort left between us. My fear will never totally go away, but the friendship will survive it.

DRIVING HOME

For a while the world of waking felt like the foreign
place, only arrived at after a long journey. I hesitated
at the border. You will know what I mean, that
moment of suspension between sleep and waking,
when we feel in sleep we've been far away.
—Kevin Oderman

I'm awake by five, anxious to get the good-bye over
with. I shower and get the last of my things together before waking Mot.
"I'm going now," I whisper, leaning over his head on the pillow. It's the
first time I've crossed the invisible barrier between his side of the cabin
and mine in all the time we've been here.

He walks groggily to the porch with me, rubbing his eyes like he's surprised to see that it's still dark, but he doesn't suggest I put off leaving.

"I left the key in the drop box by the office, but you don't have to leave
until eleven. Feel free to go back to bed. I just need to get on the road."

I step off the porch and turn back to face him, car keys in my hand. He
looks down at me, takes my face in his good hand, and kisses me lightly
on the forehead. "Drive safely," he says, and then, looking over the top of
my head at the darkened horizon, "I think I would love you if They let me
feel love. This is probably the closest I'll get."

I smile and get into my car. It's a long drive home. As I pull away, Mot's
still standing on the porch, staring out at the big sky.

It takes discipline to keep from watching Mot grow smaller in the rearview mirror, not to let myself drift into questions about his safety and well-being once I am gone. A small stone Buddha my mother had asked me to give Mot has been hiding instead in my glove box. I didn't give it to him because I was afraid it would add Buddha to his burden, and there are already enough gods pushing him around. Even the gentle ones become thugs in his singular theology. When I stop for gas, I take out the Buddha and put it on the dashboard. It reminds me that all of this—the reality I share with the cashier at the gas station, the one I share with Scotti, even the one I think of as my singular understanding of the world—is an illusion, not really any more true than the world of fallen gods and dead aunts I have just left behind. I hold this thought, hoping that it makes leaving less an act of abandonment than it feels.

I call Scotti as soon as I'm far enough along I-40 to have set the cruise control and let my mind settle into the weary work of driving. The sun rises ahead of me, setting the flat horizon ablaze, but for Scotti it's an hour later and he's already out of bed and walking the dogs. There are three of them: mine, his, and his dead mother's. We haven't been married long enough for them to be ours.

"Hey, I'm on the road home," I say, trying hard to sound excited instead of tired and a little sad. "I'm hoping to make it to Nashville tonight and then I should be home in time for dinner tomorrow."

"Is the car running okay?" he asks. "Did you remember to check the oil before you left Amarillo?"

I say "of course," but I don't say that it was Mot who did the checking, going through his own version of Scotti's careful preparations to send me out into the world. "The gas tank is full, the satellite phone is working, and I have the maps all arranged on the passenger seat."

"Well, be careful and don't speed, but get home soon."

"I'll be there tomorrow afternoon."

"I want you back in one piece," he says, and he doesn't laugh.

For Scotti, the danger was never that I would run away from home or be hurt by Mot, who he agreed seemed harmless enough. It was always that I'd end up stranded somewhere and need rescuing. And so before I left, Scotti had taken my car to the service station and mucked around with the oil, transmission fluid, the battery, and the hoses. He had double-checked the mountains of maps and guidebooks from AAA and hidden an old satellite phone, one that would get reception even where my cell would not, under the passenger seat. He had tucked into my glove box one of those hammers that will break the windshield if a car goes into a large body of water, and then he had packed my trunk with gallons of distilled water in case I got stranded in the desert.

I have to drive through fire to get home. In Arkansas, I watch long, sinewy bolts of lightning hit a distant spot on the horizon. Twenty miles west, thick smoke hangs over the highway and state policemen in face masks wave us into a small town near the Tennessee border, a long snake of cars winding down a two-lane country road while the forest combusts. The air smells of ozone and burnt pine tar. A week of magical thinking has reshaped me into someone who finds augury in the black smoke.

Mot's mental illness infuses everything with meaning. I've spent a week immersed in the unreal. It takes work to pull myself back into the world of simple cause and effect. *Sure, Moloch and Dubja are losers—I mean, if they weren't, they wouldn't be here—but I've seen them make lightning bolts shoot out of the sky.* It's hard to move from one place to the other, to see the lightning and the fire as nothing more than the normal weather of a western summer.

I'm not good at driving long distances by myself. If Scotti isn't with me, I usually stay within six hundred miles of home. Amarillo is fourteen hundred miles from Morgantown. The drive was hard on the way down, but it's worse on the way back. Torrential rains force me to the shoulder every few hundred miles. I'm not used to the flatness, to the way the wind pushes the car sideways on wet, unsheltered roads, to streaks of lightning that arc across the sky and set forests ablaze twenty miles away. My fatigue makes these minor challenges feel insurmountable.

I'd planned to stop on the other side of Nashville the first night, but I don't make it farther into Tennessee than Jackson. I stay at a hotel that costs as much as a whole week at the cabin, not because it's the only one I can find but because I'm too exhausted for thin walls and highway sounds. I need quiet, a good mattress, room service, and a clean bathroom that I don't have to share with other people's children. I'm not beyond finding

comfort in things: the Egyptian cotton sheets that smell of starch, the soft-
ness of the eiderdown comforter, the well-cooked meal served on china
with a linen napkin.

I'm pulling myself together comfort by comfort. In the Jackson Hy-
att, there are no angry gods to appease or hidden meanings in the nightly
news. Muscles uncoil, stretch, and relax. Only now, in the bland luxury of
a hotel room halfway between Mot and home, do I realize how worn out
I am. I perfume my bathwater even though I'm not leaving the room until
morning. For the first time in a week, I sleep in a nightgown instead of my
clothes.

I am alone but not lonely. This is something Mot understands and
Scotti never will: the need for time away from everyone, even those I love.
The quiet of the room calms me as much as its comforts.

                I have a history of letting homeless people live in
my spare rooms; Mike has been living with us for more than a year. He has
a quick mind and a chance. The first, Wilbur, was an old man I brought
home from the shelter where I worked in college because his doctors told
us he had only weeks to live. In the fifteen years between Wilbur and Mike,
others have stayed in whatever space I could find for them: a family who
was told they'd lose their child unless they moved out of the school bus
they'd converted into a home, an old college friend who somehow never
made it past bagger at the local supermarket, the troubled teenage daughter of a friend, and for one cold and rainy night, a drunken, rambling old
woman who had known Wilbur and thought maybe I'd let her stay, too.
Scotti and I gave Mot a bed as well, though Mike was living in the extra
room and all we could provide for Mot was a cot on the back porch. He
did his best to be good company at the dinner table, to make friends with
Scotti, and to find ways to be useful. He helped me plant the garden and
taught me how to prune the apple trees. "Thanks," he said often. "It's
nice to be around people who live a normal life. It lets me know it's still
possible, that it could happen for me." But ten days of it was all he could
bear. As soon as his Social Security check was deposited in his checking
account, he left for Amarillo.

For these temporary housemates I don't do anything but open the door,
get out the extra blankets, and offer a bed. I don't know how to turn people who can't make it on their own into people who can. The only thing I

gave Wilbur was a comfortable place to die; the rest simply stayed a while and then went back to their difficult lives, better rested but essentially unchanged. Mike may be the first to leave on his way to something better, but if he does that will be all his own doing. He was a regular at Friendship Room when I met him, homeless and trying to get ahead of the uncontrollable epilepsy that left him disoriented for days after every seizure. He was one of the few people who offered to help when it was time to clean up for the day, and he's big, so I hired him as a program assistant—one of the positions meant to be filled by consumers of the agency's services, and the first job he has had in years. Diligent if a little plodding, he has been willing to put himself between me and whoever is causing trouble. He moved in with us after getting thrown out of the homeless shelter. It simply didn't work for him to be staff at the drop-in center and a resident of Bartlett House. The other homeless men were always picking fights or trying to get him in trouble with the shelter staff, as if to say, Don't get above your station, boy. One of the saddest realizations of my time at Friendship Room is that the downtrodden would rather kill their own than see one of their ranks get ahead of the poverty and desperation. Because I had put Mike in this difficult position, Scotti and I agreed it was only right to give him a way out of it. He has been living with us for eight months now. I believe it's a sin to have empty rooms while people live on the streets, and Scotti and I share a desire to find ways to be helpful to others in need. Perhaps because we are both, in our own ways, so very needful.

I can't say what it is that Scotti needs, other than for me to be a better wife, because he would say that he's not needy. I, on the other hand, am deeply aware that I am. I need constant affirmation that I'm not a bad person, that I do more good than harm in the world, that I'm not making things worse for everybody. This need makes me tentative, awkward. I'm never certain exactly how I fit into the scheme of things. I am always afraid of what my mistakes will cost other people. I only know that I've gone far enough out of my way to be good when it becomes apparent that I've actually gone too far.

For all the difficulty of being married, I recognize the wonder of having met the only other person in the world who could see the necessity of offering Mike a place to live, and it was Scotti's work with Rita that first drew me to him. At the time, the community of service providers in which I worked saw him as something of a miracle worker because Rita, unlike everyone else we knew with a severe, chronic mental illness, was getting better. And not in small ways. When he'd taken on her case, she lived in a back ward of the state psychiatric hospital, drugged to the point of immobility. Whenever she'd been released and the medication lessened, she'd pulled her hair out until she was bald and burned hateful words into her skin with matches and lit cigarettes. Now, she had a job and an apartment. Eventually, she would go on to own her own house and enroll in the university. We service providers wanted all of our clients to work with Scotti. What we didn't know then was that he couldn't take any other clients because it took many hours a day of direct support to bring Rita as far as she had come. He had no time for other clients, and I was beginning to believe he also had no time for a wife.

It has been our commitment to making the world an easier place for people living harder lives than our own that has bound us together. Now that my commitment is wavering, that bond is being tested. I've come to the place where I can care about only a few of the people I meet at Friendship Room—Mot, Mike, Rita, and a couple of others. I would rather be done with the rest. Scotti still wants to be a hero, and mostly these heroics make me tired. He believes that if he saves Rita he will have made the world a fundamentally better place. I have begun to doubt that the world can be changed at all, much less through such a singular improvement, and I am now certain that the outcome isn't grand enough to be worth the sacrifices we make in working toward it. At least, it isn't worth it to me.

This trip to Amarillo is the first time I've approached the thing backwards, that I've been the one asking for a place to rest. Mot and I both knew that I made this trip to get out of Morgantown, and away from my job, almost as much as to visit him. That I'm trying to save myself, not him. The brother of the man who attacked me has started standing outside Friendship Room instead of coming inside—not every day, but often enough that I expect him each time I walk out of the building. I don't know if he's there to threaten me or if he's waiting on a bus. But he used to say hello, and now he stares me down.

Mot is the sort of person I expected to find when I took the job at Friendship Room. I'd imagined that my job was to find the resources to provide people with a way out of homelessness. What I do instead—provide coffee and a warm, dry place for people to sleep off, trade, or arrange to buy street drugs and arbitrate bitter disputes over who ate how many cookies or left the bathroom a mess—isn't noble or rewarding. It would have been a good thing, spending my days making life more livable for people who are surviving more dangerous worlds than mine in surprising, even ingenious ways. So I pour all the hopes I had for the job into my friendship with Mot, to see whether the smaller project of making one life better—my own—is possible.

One of the first stories Mot told me was of being in Turkey on September 11, 2001. He was in a bar, he said, drinking the one Scotch he allowed himself at the end of every week, a limit imposed more by economy than by any concern about drunkenness.

"All of a sudden, everyone got really quiet and just stared at the TV," he said. "And I looked and thought, *Oh, great, another disaster movie? Don't these goons get enough disaster over here in their own country? Sheesh! Who wants to watch a thing like that?* and went back to my Scotch. All of a sudden the old men in the bar were putting their arms around my shoulder, buying me drinks, talking to me in rapid-fire Turkish, which of course didn't make any sense to me. Normally, it would have made me nervous and I'd have had to leave, but in Turkey everyone was always mistaking me for someone famous. Musta been some trick of Jack's. So I just let the old codgers buy me whiskey and think whatever they wanted."

He'd taken out his wallet then and given me a Turkish coin from the little zippered pouch on the outside. "Here, you keep this," he'd said. Later, he would also give me a ten lekë note from Albania and a package of poppy seeds from the Ukraine that he thought might actually grow opium poppies. He produced each as proof of his unlikely stories of travel, but I don't know why he offered them as gifts instead of simply showing them to me. I was, after all, perfectly willing to believe him without any proof. We'd established that during our first conversation. And other people, I knew, would be smugly certain either that he was lying or that the travels were part of his delusion. Still, I kept them. I carry the ten lekë note in my billfold and sometimes pull it out for the same sort of proof when I tell his stories.

"Anyway," he said, putting his wallet back in his pocket, "it took two days of seeing the same thing over and over for it to sink into my stupid brain that the pictures were real, that some bleep-up had actually blown up the World Trade Center. By then, I knew I had to get back to the U.S. I mean, it wasn't a good time for anybody to be abroad, but especially a guy like me, a kook who can't stand people around him much, because everyone wanted to be around me all of a sudden. They either wanted to buy me drinks or yell at me for being an American." He sighed and shook his head. "I mean, I understand why everyone is so angry at us. All you'd have to do is leave the country for a little while and you'd understand, too." He told me he'd been stuck in Europe for another month or so because there were no flights back to the United States with empty seats, and he could afford to fly only on standby tickets. So he had hidden in a bombed-out Italian monastery, living on what he could forage from a few nearby farms and weekly trips to the local market.

I listened to Mot's story but didn't tell him my own. That I had moved from New York City to Morgantown on September 9, 2001, and that I'd watched the towers fall on a conference room television surrounded by strangers because it was the first day of the job I'd moved to take. That those strangers had crowded around me like the old men in his Turkish bar until I'd had to go into the bathroom to hide because, like him, I wanted to go unnoticed.

Most of the people who spend their days at Friendship Room are street punks whose presence brought new dangers into my world, and as a result my job had quickly stopped meeting my criteria for good works. Mostly, I made it easier for them to be junkies and petty thieves, providing a place to sleep off a bender or trade psychiatric medications in the bathroom. Their choices robbed their own lives of meaning and, for a while, robbed mine as well. I've spent years championing the dignity of those who live on our margins. If I'm wrong, if there is no dignity, then I've built a large part of my life around a beautiful lie. Faced with this distressing possibility, I've turned to the more concrete possibility of making a real difference in Mot's life, in Mike's, for some small proof that I'm not a fool.

This isn't something I can tell Mot. It would frighten him; a man lugging around two unwanted Jesuses doesn't like to be asked to save anyone. I'm never certain that I'm not doing a selfish, harmful thing to him by encouraging our friendship. His life is hard but one he is able to live, and I'm asking him to change things for my sake. I've had to cajole him into keeping the friendship intact when the Others have told him to break off all contact with me, as they often do. I don't know what it costs him to agree.

Mot says that it's good for him to have company and that it makes him feel more solid to be the one who is asked for help instead of the one asking. But he also says that the *Big Guys Upstairs* punish him for letting me tag along, for telling me that they exist, and for sharing the stories of his life. I don't know. Maybe I've been touristing misery, visiting his difficult life to gain perspective on the tiny discomforts of my own. As I drift off to sleep in my hotel room, I try to think of one thing that will be easier for him tomorrow because I was there, but I can't. He's sleeping in a car tonight, with angry gods and hidden meanings everywhere, and I'm back to freshly laundered sheets and eiderdown.

In the morning, it takes me a long time to figure out exactly where I am and why I'm here. In the first few moments of waking, I search the room for Mot or Scotti, uncertain which of them should be here but very surprised to find myself alone. I'm frightened when I can't find either one of them.

I was thirty-nine when I moved in with Scotti two years ago, and even in those first few months I thought maybe I had made a mistake, maybe I was too old to learn to be a wife. I'd lived with other people in the decade between this marriage and my last, but always in my own place and on my own terms. But my husband is a force of nature, a self-described wrecking ball careening through life, shaping the landscape to suit his needs. He can be wildly generous. But he can also spend hours fretting, and on those days it's important to walk softly and turn off all the lights when leaving a room. Living with him has meant learning to read the first hour of his waking the way you read the color of the sunrise to know if the day will be clear. It took me a long time to learn the trick of this and even longer to understand that he has had to learn to read my weather as well. Sometimes the need to read him still chafes, but this morning I miss the way the reading grounds me, gives me an understanding of how the day will go.

With Mot, the whole world changes minute by minute with only the subtlest of outward signs. Making the days work has been less forecasting and more prophesying. Like a pythoness, I've had to tune my senses to every tremor in the rock, every drift of smoke in the air. I'm exhausted from watching for the minute shifts in tone and expression that mark the appearance of the *Big Guys Upstairs*.

Now, this morning, I'm living in a world of mysteries. I've spent so many days listening for the choking sound in Mot's throat that is *Moloch*, looking to see if his eyes are focused on something I can't see, that I can't stop looking for the shadows of things I know aren't there. It feels possible that the *Others* have followed me to this hotel room. I'm looking for hints that things are okay. Signs I can get only from Mot, who isn't here. It takes me almost half an hour on the phone with Scotti to get back into the now, to get out of bed and begin the second day's drive.

MOT FROM AFAR

*If I give all I possess to the poor and surrender my body
to the flames, but have not love, I gain nothing.*
—Corinthians 13:3

The morning I go back to work is sunny and pleasant. The few people who wander into Friendship Room sit quietly reading or playing Spades. The pile of mail on my desk is manageable. I'm behind enough to be busy but not overburdened. For a few minutes, I imagine that the time away has made me someone who can now do this job with renewed energy. That maybe I should rescind my resignation. But not an hour into my first day back, I start to get complaints about how things have been managed in my absence: staff reportedly smoking marijuana in the office, offensive movies shown, the coffee pot allowed to run dry. I don't believe the first accusation and don't care about the second or third. I look at the tedium of the next few months and cannot understand why I've come back here at all. So I can turn a deaf ear to the suffering of people I've grown to distrust and, worse, dislike? Mot's friendship had filled the space between the reality of the days here and what I hoped for when I first started this job. It was the only thing that had kept me afloat in this otherwise miserable place. Together we were a tiny oasis of words and ideas. We were kind and truthful and compassionate. We were not at all like the world around us.

But I left Mot in Amarillo, knowing that the *Big Guys Upstairs* would drag him back down into the hole they'd dug for him. I get an email from him midafternoon as I'm finishing up the paperwork generated by all the complaints about how things were done during my time away.

> Sure, when we are together life is good and on the brink of springing eternal. When we part we are left with a bit of us and the rest of what we usually are. With me it is a continuation of figuring and coping with life and hereafter. With you, your job, your domestic, and most of all your on-going family involvement; of course the likable turf of Morgantown and friends and familiars helps. The simple version.
>
> BEWARE OF WHAT'S HAPPENING HERE. I have gleaned (speaking of 'accidents'), lots of help over the years, there seems to be something that doesn't want us to get completely totaled without some clues. How it works when you are away is filled with false impressions; little if any to do with me, plenty to do with the program. Of course your butties (really—the Eng novelists of the 1800's spelled it thus), the used to be girls upstairs are now cluing you in on how and why this can or cannot be. And so it is—but that is only a small portion of what the complete program is. I have only 10 minutes so I'll tune off and tune in later for a reply.

Mot and I had seen this coming. We'd planned for it. I'd spent a lot of time convincing him that we'd get through it best if he'd use the cell phone. Still, I'm surprised and relieved when he actually picks up. He has read my reply, a long and apparently completely misguided rebuttal of everything I'd thought he'd said. It's impossible to know, ever, if I have misunderstood him or if the delusions have shifted away from the pointy end of my logic, unassailable. But once we're on the phone we seem to be okay again. "Voices help," he says. "I can't listen to you and to them at the same time." Thus begins the ritual of the two o'clock phone call.

On my end, it goes like this: make a cup of tea, grab a stack of already finished paperwork, and tell Mike that I'm going next door to work and shouldn't be disturbed unless there is a fight, fire, or board member in the room. Go next door to the office and spread the papers around me as if I'm working on them, in case someone actually comes for me. Lock the door. Sit cross-legged on the couch. Call. Mot tells me that on his end, it works this way: suppress the urge to throw the phone away first thing in the morning. Spend an hour charging the phone in the small-appliance aisle at Walmart. Make sure the phone is turned on. Make sure again. Worry for a while that Morgantown is an hour behind, not an hour ahead of, Amarillo time. Remember having read somewhere that cell phones give people brain cancer. Get sick of the phone and throw it into the backseat. Drive to the library. Check email. Go out to the car and get the phone. Go back into the library and read until the phone rings. Stand under the only tree outside the library for some shade while talking.

Mot begins every call by telling me how much he hates the phone, even on the day he then says, "I woke up last night at around three and couldn't get back to sleep, so I just sat with the phone. I can see how a fellow might get to like these things, knowing you could call someone if you really wanted to." Mot says that having someone to talk to every day makes things better, but it's always a battle between him and the *Big Guys Upstairs*.

The day I got back to town, I posted a request for a wireless-enabled laptop to Freecycle.com, a Web resource for finding people to take your old junk off your hands or to ask for things people are likely to have lying around. I've used Freecycle to give away four dozen blue binders and to gather old magazines and scraps of yarn for a crafts project. Asking for a laptop is a bit like going to a flea market in search of an Hermès scarf. But having found hope in my friendship with Mot, I allow myself to look for it in all sorts of unlikely places.

A local poet comes miraculously to our aid and donates a laptop that exceeds my wildest expectations. It has a 17-inch screen, 128 megs of video memory, and a wireless modem. It will give Mot constant access to email, Google Books and Project Gutenberg, and streaming music—all things that he has said he wants, that he thinks would help. It's so good that I feel guilty sending it off to an uncertain future. Mot has been able to cope with the phone so far, but we're fighting history. At some point, I feel certain, the *Big Guys Upstairs* will toss everything that ties him to me away, even if they have to throw him down the stairs and into darkness to do it.

I send the computer General Delivery, which catches the attention of the guy in the post office. "You really shouldn't ship something so valuable this way, you know," he says, and the way he says it suggests that I had better come up with a good story, fast, or the laptop will end up in his apartment. "I'm sending it to my husband. He's a paleontologist, and he's out on a dig in the desert. His laptop died, so the university is loaning him this one." There. I've now attached it to a professor and named the university as its owner, making it harder to steal.

It must have worked, because the laptop made it to Mot only a few days later. Once he has it, Mot and I are in almost constant contact during the day. The first email he sends me is full of hopefulness.

> A new experience for me, this is. I've never asked a girl for anything. I suppose I should stop saying girl. This has the possibility for fulfilling a lost part of life and its purpose—even late in the day. Obviously I'm uncertain about results—have doubts—going forward, though, seems the best plan. The bug-a-boos are the habits, concepts, past success, and the ways we have traditionally gotten along. The great difference is partnership and newness. Mainly a chance to create as we go.

Mot moves out of the Walmart parking lot and takes up residence outside a local bookstore with a free Wi-Fi connection. We learn to use Skype because our chatter is breaking me at twenty-five cents a minute. Prepaid cell phones are a crime—a tax on human contact for the poor. He spends his nights reading detective novels he has downloaded from Google Books and listening to Spike Jones on Rhapsody. By day he sits in the bookstore, charging the battery and nursing a cup of coffee. "I've noticed," he says during the first week, "that people treat me differently now. I mean, nobody thinks you're homeless when you're lugging a hunk of junk like this around with you." I like the computer most for the way it transforms how he is seen. Once he has it, bookstore employees no longer ask him to leave after an hour or so, he says, and everyone is friendlier. The laptop camouflages the broken sunglasses from Dollar Tree, the dirt on the cuffs of his pants and shirt, the fact that he pays for his cup of coffee with nickels and dimes.

I'm loved by people who work to make certain that I know it. My husband has survived the adjustments required by my quirkiness and come around to loving me in spite of them, or so I hope. My mother loves all of her children with an animal ferocity. She has loved me well enough that no one has ever been able to break my heart. My father loves me in the baffled sort of way that a certain kind of man loves his grown daughters, not quite sure how to show it now that there aren't skinned knees and broken toys to fix, but steadily and with pride. Even my sixteen-year-old stepdaughter will sometimes fold herself onto the couch beside me and say, "Love you, Lady," without wanting money or the car. This, I'm told by other stepmothers, approaches the miraculous. And, like anyone with enough of a thing, I'm careless in giving it away.

It's a small thing for me to say the word love. I do it easily and to many people. I love Mot now the way I loved my friends when I was younger, with the sort of passionate dedication that comes from reading the same books, pondering the same ideas, and sitting up all night talking. It has been years since I spent time on the phone chatting about the everyday, a habit I lost when work became the center of my life and the things I had to talk about interested no one but my office mates. It feels good to have a friend who cares about the small things that make up my days now: how the garden is growing, the tedious dramas of Friendship Room, even what I'm making for dinner. And one day it happens, and without a thought I sign an email with "Love" instead my habitual "Peace."

But it's not a small thing for Mot to receive a letter that ends in "Love," and I should have been more careful. I notice I have done it only when I go back and reread what I've written, looking for a reason he hasn't written back within a few hours, as is his habit. Part of being Mot's friend is taking the time to find the meaning in things that would be trivial in any of my other friendships. It's never safe to assume that things are as they appear, that maybe he got busy with something else or has changed his routine.

Nothing in the note itself seems extraordinary. I wrote about having tried a new kind of tea, something buried under the ground for months, and finding it too much like drinking dirty laundry. Not much else, really. I have to read it three times before I even notice the word love. I decide it's not something that should be taken back. Better to be patient, to wait to see what happens next.

I have my answer the next morning. Unable to write the word himself, Mot has closed his letter by quoting mine, ending with "Love, S/mot." The email itself is a long and rambling riff on the idea of making tea from dirty clothes. He adds it to his growing menu of Car Cuisine, a list that also includes Cargonzola, cheese made by leaving milk too long in the back-seat, and Accidental Salami, the result of letting a tube of hamburger from

Walmart sit for weeks in the trunk. On the phone later, he tells me the S/ is there because he didn't want to totally delete my name. Doing so seemed like inviting the *Big Guys Upstairs* to make something of the erasure.

S/mot becomes our new word. It means me, or Mot, or the two of us collectively. I send him S/motly cartoons from the *New Yorker*, and he tells me that the Max Brand book he has been reading is surprisingly S/motish for a western. Like everything, we play it into the ground. Once we've used it up, we move on to anagrams.

He starts the game, signing an email *A Hat Roams*. It takes me several puzzled readings to realize it's made out of the combined letters of our names. I reply as Mao Trash, liking the counter-counterrevolutionary sound of it. We send anagrams back and forth, eventually devolving into groupings of letters that seem as if they could be words but aren't. After a while, this becomes how I can tell the good days from the bad ones; letters written when he's under siege are signed only "mot" or not signed at all. On good days, he's Moat Rash or Ha! To Arms!

We go on like this, happily, for two weeks. There are a few confused conversations, a troubling email or two. "*When a person is an open book, realizing that even the peer group is moving away, what can you do? I suppose I must continue to resist, try to get a handle on the night. Reports of my death greatly exaggerated (Twain). The deck has been stacked, this I can't abide. If I lose stand by for a new Jesus, I'll try to make sure you get special consideration. mot.*" But for the most part, things are light. We've already made plans for a second visit, this time in Oklahoma City. I'm trying to very slowly move him eastward, hoping to eventually convince him to come back to Morgantown at least long enough to see a doctor and get a definitive answer about the cause of his paralysis. I don't say this, though. I tell him I want to go to Oklahoma City for the *pho*, a Vietnamese dish I love but can't get in Morgantown. I forward Mot a recent column from the *New York Times* by the Frugal Traveler, Matt Gross. Mot and I had been following his journeys across the United States, looking for likely places to visit. Mot thinks Gross's account of the Kentucky Bourbon Trail seems worthy of a trip into the land of sour mash, but I don't think his car could hold up on such a long drive.

We had driven past a scary, seedy *pho* restaurant on our way to and from the KOA in Amarillo. Almost every day I suggested we risk it and then chickened out. It was push and pull for me, my favorite food but served in a restaurant that looked like a crime scene waiting to happen. The white adobe building had barred windows, an aging Mexican cantina facade, and a parking lot that was empty until ten at night, when it filled up with old sedans that had jacked-up back ends and custom paint jobs. It had the look of a place better known for its backroom cockfights than for its food.

Mot relents to my enthusiasm for Oklahoma City and the possibility of *pho*. He's uncertain about the idea of Vietnamese food, thinks his old friend Fahey wouldn't like it if he fraternized with Charlie, but in the end his indulgent streak wins out. We set a date, book a cabin at the KOA east of the city, and send each other likely routes via MapQuest. And then, just as our plans are finalized, Mot disappears. I get this cryptic email and then nothing.

> Arrgh, a miserable night after a good day. seems to be a cycle. speaking of which they had you sounding like aunt minette (the eyetalian one) on the phone. i told you there is a lot of devious activity up stairs, also a lot of jew haters. a lot of investment has gone into this mess over here, so beware. so the way i feel i have to take a breather from all contact— maybe join a—i don't know . . . might contact after a month or so.

I try to call, but of course the phone is turned off. I send a panicked email and then a sensible one, saying that I will write every day, a note to let him know that the door is open. I work very hard at sounding calm. In reality, I'm not. As soon as he's gone, the walls of Friendship Room start closing in on me. I check my email several times an hour, hoping for some response. I call his cell every day at two, and then I check the online payment page I use to buy his minutes to see if he has used any of them to listen to his messages. He hasn't.

I poll my friends. Half think he's gone for good, half think I'll hear from him in a couple of weeks. Their lack of agreement doesn't help things any, and they are equally divided on the question of the daily email. Either they think it's a nice gesture or they believe it will scare him into permanent silence. In the end, I decide that having said I will write, I will write. If it's a risk either way, I choose to do the things I've said I will, and hope that constancy proves a virtue.

WILBUR

Oh Death! Oh Death!
Won't you spare me over to another year?
Please spare me over to another year.
—Traditional

On the day I met Wilbur, the snow was coming
down so hard and fast I had to walk to work. My battered old car and its
bald tires couldn't be trusted on icy pavement, and already the snow lay
in drifts as high as the front bumper. I was pulling a double at Bartlett
House—8:00 a.m. to midnight—and figured that even if I could get the car
there, I'd have to leave it when my shift was over. The weather report called
for another foot or so of snow. So, bundled in my mother's hand-me-down
parka, my roommate's too-big snow boots, and the kaffiyeh I wore then
as both a scarf and a political statement, I walked the few miles between
home and the homeless shelter through the beginnings of what would
come to be known as the Storm of the Century, the Great Blizzard of 1993.

Bartlett House was new then, with only a handful of dormitory rooms,
a large communal area for watching television and serving meals, an industrial kitchen, and three offices. The shelter had a men's room and a
women's room, each with two toilets and two showers, and another half
bath behind the locked door of the general staff office. We had room on
the bed assignment sheet for forty people. By the time I got to work that
morning, forty-seven people had checked in for the day.

"Police are bringing everybody in," said Rich, who had worked the overnight shift. "Not just the guys off the riverbank, either. I mean everybody." He gestured to the hallway packed with people milling around, pointing to one guy in particular. Melvin. We'd kicked him out of the shelter a few months before when, after the other residents had complained of a terrible smell coming from his bunk, we'd discovered several decomposing squirrel carcasses and a hunting knife tucked inside his rucksack. He'd refused to give up either, saying the food we served was full of poison and he preferred to eat what he could kill on his own. Even the police were a little wary of Melvin, who was rumored now to be living off feral cats and roadkill in a sewer pipe near the Walmart.

"Did they take his knife away?" I asked.

"Said they did," Rich answered, in a way that suggested that there was a good chance they hadn't.

"The cops said we couldn't turn anybody away until the weather breaks." Rich handed me the bed assignment sheet and the cordless phone, our only link to outside help in an emergency. "I ran out of blankets. I've been giving out the towels and extra mattress pads, but we're almost out of those, too. There's maybe a little room left on the floors in rooms four and five, but other than that, we're past full."

He took me into the day room, where the regular residents had set up camp in the chairs and the new folk were left to lean against walls or crouch on the floor. In a far corner, the riverbank men stood in a tight knot around the coffee pot. "I think they have a bottle, but I'd let them keep it," said Rich. "I don't know about you, but I wouldn't want to deal with Bugs and Cecil going through DTs on top of everything else."

I nodded. These men never came to the shelter willingly. Drinking wasn't a choice for them, and Bartlett House had a strict rule against it. But Rich was right. Half drunk, they'd be manageable. Dry, they'd be sick and mean. "Michelle already called and said she can't make it in tonight because they've closed the highway. I'd stay, but I can't leave my dad alone all weekend. I left a message with William. He's not due till tomorrow morning, but maybe he can come early. Otherwise, I'm afraid you're on your own until morning."

I stood in the office with Rich as he bundled up to leave. "What do you mean, I'm on my own?" Usually, the four-to-midnight shift was staffed by two shelter workers, and even on slow evenings there was more than enough to keep two people busy. This would not be a slow evening.

"I mean nobody else is coming. Donna lives too far out of town to get here in this weather, and Rose . . ." His voice trailed off. Rose, the executive director, was terrified of the clients. We both knew she wouldn't come in even if she lived right across the street. "Look," he said, "it won't be so bad. Get some of the regulars to help with dinner, and whatever you make, make a lot of it. Get them full and sleepy." He shook his head. "If things start to get hairy, call the cops. Even if it's something you'd normally let slide. We'll probably have sixty or so people in here by nightfall. You'll need to get anyone who might be trouble out of here before the roads get so bad even the police can't make it down."

The idea that we'd be cut off even from the police was frightening, particularly with so many people forced inside by the storm who usually avoided the shelter because of its rules.

"What do I do if there's trouble and the police can't come?" I asked. Rich had worked at the shelter for a little more than two years; I'd been there for only one. He was older, more sure of himself, and when we worked together, he was the one who intervened when the residents got out of hand.

"Don't let that happen." Rich looked over the bed assignment sheet and put check marks by a few of the names. "Look, these guys would probably stick up for you in a pinch. It's against every rule, but if there's real trouble and the police can't get here, ask them to help you out." He then circled at least twice as many names as he'd checked. "These are the guys you need to watch out for," he said. "If things get really bad, make the police send officers down on foot. If they tell you they don't have anybody, tell them you're going to start kicking people out. If they still won't come . . ." He trailed off. "I don't know what you should do if they still won't come. Lock yourself in the office, maybe, and at least make dispatch stay on the phone. Make sure you write down everything. We don't really have a protocol for dealing with a situation like this." He opened one of the file-cabinet drawers and pulled out a stack of blank incident reports. "You may have to cover your ass if things go badly tonight. If anything makes it into the papers, Rose will be looking to fire someone to appease the board. Write people up for even small things, so you can justify whatever you have to do." He shook his head. "Sorry I can't stay. Good luck."

Rich left. I gathered a small corps of long-term residents, and together we worked out a strategy for dealing with the demands of the sudden influx of so many people. Traveling Jack and Cat-Eye sat guard near the door in exchange for the privilege of coming back into the shelter after a few beers later that night. They escorted the people who came in throughout the day back to the kitchen so I could find them a place to sleep and write their names in the margins of the bed assignment sheet. Rita and Star peeled fifty pounds of potatoes, Errol boiled them in batches, and a woman called Granny Lynn mashed them with commodity butter and tins of evaporated milk. Carthelius helped me pull pounds and pounds of ground venison out of the freezers and defrost it in the microwave. Granny Lynn mixed it with powdered eggs, dehydrated onions, ketchup, and cornflakes, making four giant meatloaves in five-gallon metal steam-table trays. Everyone in the kitchen was sworn to secrecy. The venison was the only thing we had enough of to feed this crowd, but it turns out beggars can be choosers. The venison had been languishing in the freezers for months because when we told the residents what it was, most of them refused to eat it.

Right before dinner Cat-Eye walked in with a sick old man who was wearing a light jacket and torn sneakers with no laces and who carried a sheaf of paperwork in a wet brown paper bag. There was a bloodied bandage at his throat, and his eyes were rheumy. "Cop said they found him sitting at the bus stop in front of the hospital. Says his name is Wilbur, but other than that he don't talk much." He put a hand under the old man's elbow to steady him. "Don't look so good, either." Wilbur swayed a little and then fell back into Cat-Eye's arms.

Wilbur spent the night on the floor of the office, wrapped in the least worn mattress pad I could find and my mother's old parka. I didn't sleep but sat perched in the desk chair after lights-out, listening to him breathe. It seemed possible that at some point in the night, his breathing would stop. The bag of papers turned out to be prescriptions and discharge orders, and the bloody bandage covered the place where he'd had a feeding tube until that morning. There was a tumor the size of a bread loaf hanging over the belt of his pants. Stomach cancer, he told me. "Probably won't live till spring," he'd said during the intake process, as if it were just another piece of information for the form. "But the medical card only pays for so many days in the hospital, and I guess my days must have run out this morning." He smiled and then turned his hands up in a gesture of helplessness.

Wilbur either never had been or always had been homeless, depending on how you feel about private property. He lived in the same tar-paper shack he'd been raised in, but he didn't own it. His family had been squatting on unused coal company land for three generations. He had worked odd jobs and done some jackleg coal mining, but mostly he lived off what he could grow, hunt, and—since his sixty-fifth birthday a few months before—buy with his meager Social Security check. He was country poor, and this was before Oxycontin and crystal meth destroyed what dignity came with that. He drank some but wasn't a drunk. He didn't read well but had never needed to learn. He wasn't much of a churchgoing man because the church was a long walk from his home and he'd never owned a working car, but he said his prayers and figured he was mostly right with God. His was a simple life, but one well enough lived to suit him. Or it had been, until the cancer had forced him into town.

I'd heard a lot of tragic stories in my year at Bartlett House, and I knew that almost everyone who ended up there could have avoided it if jobs doing manual labor had been easier to find. If we hadn't stopped building low-income housing. If we still believed it was the obligation of the middle class to offer a hand up to the impoverished. If we'd followed up on the promise to build full-service community mental health centers after we released the people who had been held prisoner in our system of asylums and state hospitals. But I also knew the parts of their stories that made their homelessness more than the inevitable result of a failing social welfare system: the women who used the shelter to get away from one abusive man only to leave a few weeks later with another, the old men who had to drink to get by, the young men and women who were mentally ill and augmented their craziness with street drugs but didn't take the pills that would have made them better. The people who lived here had difficult lives and complicated stories. My job was to feed them, assign them chores and beds, and keep what passed for peace among them as best I could.

Wilbur's story wasn't complicated. He was an old man from the country who had gotten by until cancer made him too weak to hunt or farm. He hadn't ended up at Bartlett House because he'd drunk himself there, squandered his money, or been caught cheating on a disability claim. No, Wilbur had ended up at Barlett House because he'd never married or had children, and kin was how a man like Wilbur got through his dying years.

———————————

William got to the shelter at a little after four the next morning, ice in his eyelashes and beard and his pants frozen stiff up to the thighs. "I'm sorry I couldn't get here earlier, but I had to walk in, and I couldn't do it until the snow died down a little." It was at least five miles from his apartment to the shelter. "I started out a little bit before two, but it was slow going."

"It's okay," I said, and it had been. "Something about the storm made everyone cooperative. There wasn't any trouble. Might be more difficult today, though, now that the novelty has worn off." I gestured to Wilbur asleep on the floor and motioned for William to come into the hallway with me. "The only scary thing was that old man. Name's Wilbur. They put him out of the hospital yesterday, and he's really sick. I was afraid he'd take a turn for the worse and there is no way an ambulance could get down here."

"I'll keep an eye on him." William and I stepped over the people sleeping in the hallways and went into the kitchen. By midnight, over sixty people had been checked in. Only the kitchen and the offices that belonged to the social worker and executive director were empty. We didn't have keys to those offices, or they'd have had people in them, too.

"I'll stay and help out until after breakfast," I said. "I can't get home, anyway, until it's light out." William nodded. "We should make a big breakfast." I got out the flour and butter and started making biscuits. William dug through the pantry for extra cans of coffee.

"Thank you for making it in," I said.

It took surprisingly little convincing to get the social worker, then the executive director, and finally the woman who administered our primary grant at the state capital to let me break every rule about client-staff interaction and take Wilbur home with me. We moved him into the empty basement apartment in my house less than two weeks after he'd been brought to the shelter by the police. Even people with long careers in social services, and the disillusionment that goes with them, understood that Wilbur's story shouldn't end at Bartlett House, and that if we allowed the rules to stop us from making sure it didn't, then we were not the good people we held ourselves out to be.

The basement apartment was a dump, even compared to the rest of my ramshackle little house. When I'd first bought the place, which had no central heating and cost less than a new car, I had rented the apartment out to a local writer, who thought it was romantically disgusting, for a hundred dollars a month. After he'd moved out, I'd left it empty with the vague plan, but neither the skill nor the money, to fix it up. The floors of the apartment were concrete poured directly on dirt, the walls crumbling drywall or exposed cinderblock. The bathroom had only a toilet and a miner's shower: a showerhead attached directly to a pipe in the ceiling over a drain in the floor. But Wilbur's shack had neither running water nor electricity, and the apartment in my basement had its own street-level entrance with a wide porch shaded by an apple tree and a row of forsythia separating it from the road, both of which seemed to bloom almost the instant the snows from the storm had melted. "I like to sit out on the porch of an evening and have me a sip of beer," Wilbur had said upon seeing the place. I understood that to mean that he would take it.

Wilbur was fastidious about his apartment. He spent his money on new curtains and a slipcover for the old sleeper sofa in the living room, big bottles of bleach and boxes of steel wool. The social worker from the shelter found him dishes, sheets, an old vacuum cleaner, and a television. The grants director from the state sent him two ferns as a housewarming gift. Virgil Peterson, one of my English professors, produced a mattress and box spring that he said were used and lying around his house but that still smelled like the plastic wrappings in which they had been packaged. Rich, the overnight shelter worker, borrowed a truck and drove Wilbur deep into Preston County to retrieve what he wanted from the tar-paper shack. Less than a month after being released from the hospital, Wilbur was as much on his feet as he had ever been.

The cancer didn't kill him by spring of that year, or the next. For as long as I lived in the little house on Hite Street, he did, too. He was rarely any trouble. Once in a while he'd go downtown and forget that since the cancer, he couldn't tolerate more than two beers. He would have four or five and then start the walk home only to discover that he was too tired to make it. The police would find him asleep on a bench in the courthouse square. When they woke him, he'd say, "Call my daughter Sarah." And the police, who knew I wasn't his child, would call and say jokingly, "We need you to come and get your father." When I'd arrive to pick him up from the station, he'd hug me and wink, as if he thought we'd really pulled one over on the Man. The police winked, too, as if we'd pulled one over on old Wilbur. And I would smile because for one of the few times in my life, I knew that nobody was getting the raw end of this deal.

On Wednesdays, when I was at school, he would let himself into my part of the house to use the old ringer washer in my kitchen and hang his clothes to dry on a line he'd strung from the apple tree to the side of the house. When the washing machine broke down, which it did every few months, he fixed it. He was handy and often came upstairs to tinker with the plumbing, the old Warm Morning heaters, the fuse box. He said he'd never owned a car, but he kept my oil changed. And although he couldn't push the lawnmower, he kept the blades sharp and made sure it was full of gas so that I could.

Every Saturday, I brought him his groceries: twenty one cans of chocolate Ensure, two Hershey's chocolate bars, and seven forty-ounce bottles of malt liquor. We'd sit on the porch for a while, or in winter stand in the kitchen, and gossip about the goings-on at the shelter. The folk who cycled in and out were as close as he had to friends since moving into town, and he would warn me when Traveling Jack was on a drinking binge and ought to be put out at night, when Pamela was off her meds and needed looking after, when there was someone new in town that he thought was up to no good and warranted a little extra scrutiny. He knew, without being told, that he shouldn't bring these friends back to the house. If they gave him grief about this, he never let on, though I imagine they did. Apartments were communal among the frequently homeless. It was bad form to have a place and not let other folk crash there. This was part of why it was so hard for them to hold on to apartments once they had them.

During his courses of chemo, I would take Wilbur to the hospital twice a week to have the little pump he wore in a fanny pack refilled. Because he got the poison so slowly, he said it never made him ill, but he refused radiation treatment after the first course. Given the odds, he didn't think the sickness it caused was worth it. "If I was a dog, it wouldn't be time to put me down, but there wouldn't be no use in taking me to the vet, neither," he would joke. He was proud of outlasting his prognosis. He refused pain medication because the doctor told him he couldn't drink while taking it, and that offended his sense of autonomy. Most nights, he said, he fell asleep while the bottle was still mostly full and dumped out the rest in the morning, but it was the principle of the thing. "Ain't nobody," he'd say, "should tell an old man he can't have himself a beer at night excepting his wife, and I never wanted me no wife."

Wilbur was accustomed to solitude. He didn't ask much, and he preferred to tinker with the car or the washing machine when I wasn't home, so early on I gave him a key to my door and an extra set of keys to the car. It never occurred to me to wonder about the wisdom of this. Because he couldn't write well, he left artifacts instead of notes: empty oil cans, the busted belt he'd replaced on the washer, sometimes in spring a bouquet of wildflowers wrapped in a paper towel on my kitchen table. That he asked so little, and was so completely trustworthy, made it easy to have him there. Very soon, we began simply to think of ourselves as neighbors, though the helpful and concerned sort that even then seemed something of an anachronism. A blessing, really.

After I finished college, in the summer that I was twenty nine—long after Wilbur should have been dead, according to his doctor—I sold the house and moved to Alabama. I felt guilty leaving Wilbur behind, with nobody to drive him to chemotherapy or do his shopping, and once asked him if he wanted to come with me. No, he said, he liked where he was just fine, and he could get along, he promised. There were the ladies at Christian Help for rides to the doctor or shopping trips, and although they wouldn't buy his malt liquor, he felt certain that he could find someone who would. So I knocked five thousand dollars off the price of the house and sold it to some friends with the understanding that Wilbur could stay there, rent free, for as long as he lived. He died two weeks later, sitting in an old armchair that he'd found in a neighbor's trash and moved onto the porch that afternoon.

I think about Wilbur often during the weeks that Mot is out of touch. Wilbur's needs had been so modest, and the rewards for meeting them so great, that even the bureaucrats had seen the sense in letting me take him in. There had never been any question of saving him because he was already past saving when he arrived. And it was an easy thing to give an already dignified man an opportunity to die a dignified death.

Giving Wilbur a place to stay also gave my life dignity it hadn't had until then. It gave credibility to my hippie-chick way of being in the world, showed that it was more than a patchouli-scented pose. Morgantown is a small place, the university community even more so. I sometimes had to say to my professors, "I'm going to miss class today to take Wilbur to chemo." I became, then, that girl with the old man from the homeless shelter in her basement instead of just another Birkenstock-wearing dropout come back to seek shelter in the English Department. That isn't why I did it, but it made it easier to *keep* doing it on the rare occasion when Wilbur needed more from me than I really wanted to give.

I worry that both Scotti and I understand ourselves only through the things we do for other people, that we don't know how to find meaning in the relationship we have with each other. He will leave Lucy and me at the dinner table to drive to Rita's apartment to calm her down if she's upset. I've left them both for a week and driven fourteen hundred miles to see what difference I can make in Mot's life. Neither one of us is willing to go very far out of our way for the other, though. If I'm upset, he tells me to stop being so sensitive. When he calls to ask me to come pick him up at a bar because he's had too much to drink, I'm pissy about having to get out of bed and drive a couple of miles. When I voice this fear, he says that I'm not grateful for all the things he does for me, but that I'm right about not being very kind to him. And so we can't talk about it, can't try to work through it, because it reaffirms his belief that the problem lies solely with me.

IN THE YELLOW HOUSE

Fond as we are of our loved ones, there comes at times
during their absence an unexplained peace.
—**Anne Shaw**

It's the first weekend after Mot's disappearance.
Scotti is standing on the porch talking to the college kids we have hired
to paint the house. I can't hear what's being said, but he is pointing to a
spot where the old paint has started to peel away from the wood. I watch
through the window. We are both in love with this house, its hundred-
year-old woodwork, walls at odd angles, and miner's shower in the basement. It's a nicer version of my old house on Hite Street. Tiger lilies bloom
in profusion by the front porch. Small, green bunches of grapes ripen on
their vines, promising more than double of last year's crop. I should be
out there beside him, excited about the fresh coat of paint, pointing out
the rotting wood by the cellar door, insisting that they not stand their
ladders in the flower beds. But I'm not, because this isn't my house; it's
his, and I live here only because he allows it. Our prenuptial agreement is
clear on this. I would never have chosen the bright yellow the painters are
slathering on the wood. I wanted the clapboards white and the shutters
classic dark green. But it will be yellow with too-bright, hunter-green trim
instead. What I like, Scotti finds plain. What he likes, I find tacky and em-
barrassing. And my love of the house, like my love for his daughter, holds
me hostage to his way of doing things. I can't fight for the white paint or
against letting thirteen-year-old Lucy eat nothing but pizza and chicken

nuggets without being told that this is his house, his family, and he will do what he damn well pleases.

In our first months here, we bickered over everything: the placement of family photographs (his on the walls and mantle, mine in boxes in the attic), the arrangement of the kitchen (he wanted pots up high where he didn't have to bend for them, I wanted them down low where I could reach them without climbing on a chair). Whether to keep the broken recliner from his old living room or get something new (we kept the recliner until my mother bought us a new couch and sofa as a housewarming gift). But I don't fight anymore. I'm a guest in his home, and although he insists loudly and angrily that my tally is bullshit, I have won only a single argument since we moved in two years ago. The pots are kept low enough that I can reach them, though Scotti refuses to do any of the cooking because of it. In the five years we will live in that house, he will make dinner exactly twice. I have a place to live, but it's not my home, it's someone else's. Like Mike in the basement, I'm here only as long as I don't make too much trouble.

I live in a place to which I have no legal claim and from which I could be evicted at any moment without recourse. Social workers call this *being doubled up*. It is one of the ways a person can qualify for homelessness benefits.

I'm only half here, anyway, and that fault is all my own. Maybe if I were more present, I would have a greater part in the family that is made up mostly of Scotti and Lucy. The days at Friendship Room leave me dull and numb. On good ones I stay out of bed long enough to eat dinner and watch a little TV with the two of them; on bad ones I'm in my pajamas by late afternoon. I've developed tunnel vision and the skin is sloughing off my hands, an eczema the doctor attributes to stress. She gives me Xanax, but I won't take it during working hours, afraid it will dull my senses. Touching anything hurts, and I can watch the blood move under the thin, pink skin of my palms.

I've lost control at Friendship Room and everyone knows it. Most of the violence against me is small and veiled: an intentional shove in the hallway followed by a feigned apology, an elbow to the kidney followed by a muttered, "Sorry, didn't see you there." But not all of it. An aged Marine with a fondness for Wild Irish Rose comes in falling-down drunk, and when I take him out to the second-story landing that acts as the entrance to Friendship Room and ask him to leave, he calls me a cunt and shoves me down the fire escape to the pavement below. At the grocery store, I run into a man I'd kicked out of the room for good a few months ago for beating his wife in front of the building, shattering her cheekbone and jaw. He had felt so wronged by the sanction that he had written to the board asking to be reinstated, insisting that because the altercation with his wife happened outside the room and because we had no business meddling in his domestic affairs, the punishment was unfair. He follows me down the canned goods aisle and then, in the cramped space between the meat cooler and the employee break room, sidles close and whispers, "Best not let me catch you in the parking lot, bitch. You can't do shit about nothing here."

I sit in the bathroom at Kroger for two hours, crying, waiting for the nerve to walk to the car. I'm alternately awash in self-pity and furious at myself for being such a goddamned pussy. When I finally get home, I'm too tired even to tell Scotti why I'm late. But it doesn't matter, because he hasn't noticed that I am. I unload the groceries and crawl into bed.

I speed the days along by renting movies to keep regulars in front of the television, which cuts down on the number of confrontations, if not the clandestine drug dealing. The rules against films that show drug use, explicit sex, or gratuitous violence no longer seem worth enforcing. I let whatever holds their interest play. Movies like *Saw* and *Hostel* run constantly in the background, the soundtrack to my days now the screams of women being hacked to death by madmen. But the movies keep most everyone on the couches and away from my desk, so I learn to endure them.

Only requests for practical assistance get a response from me now. I no longer listen to the constant bickering between homeless cliques or stories about abusive boyfriends. Maybe that is the secret to doing this job, or would have been if I'd learned it earlier. Ask me for something concrete or don't ask me for anything at all. This one needs a tent, that one a bus ticket home to his mother in Michigan. I make calls, wringing final donations out of the people who have been good in a pinch during my year here. I ask for sleeping bags, underwear, tarps, and backpacks but not money. Things are mine to give away. Money is not.

Friends have begun to describe me as fragile. The neighbor who shares my morning dog walk recommends that I read the book *The Gift of Fear*, and the man I sit beside in the Mennonite church I attend—an enthusiastic raw-foods bicycle evangelist—pats my hand when I cry during services. He has stopped suggesting that giving up meat might help. Instead, he has started carrying crumpled tissues and holding the hymnal so I don't have to when my hands shake. I'm not certain how I became the troubled woman who looks back at me from the bathroom mirror. This is not the hardest thing I have ever had to live through, not by a long shot. And yet, somehow, it's the one that undoes me.

A board member asks how a fumbled sexual assault could possibly have thrown me so badly. I want to say, "It wasn't his hand on my breasts, or his cock out of his pants, that did it. It was his arm across my throat. The way my vision blurred and then darkened at the edges. The feeling of my knees about to give way, and the sound of my own blood grown so loud I could no longer hear his mumbled demands. It was the sudden, awful knowledge that had the participants seen us, many of them would not have helped me." But I don't, because she isn't really asking, she's reprimanding. So I say, "I don't know. I'm sorry," and she goes away, satisfied to have gotten an apology.

I'm angry with myself for handling things so badly since the attack in the hallway. I like to think of myself as someone who soldiers on—something I get from my mother. My mother is stronger, though, and commands respect. I have neither her patience nor her gravitas, which means I can't succeed here.

I would like to be someone else, a person capable of rising to the challenges of Friendship Room. More than fear, more than self-pity, it's the inescapable fact of my failure that eats away at me. I had thought that I would be good at this job and that it would allow me to use my meager talents to make a real difference in some very difficult lives. Instead, it has broken me. I'm just waiting for permission to walk away.

Two weeks after he disappeared, Mot is back in my in-box.

> As I recently said—funny you (we) reach a place of diminished expectations and voila.

Now to try again. I had written early in the month, I guess I'll copy it verbatim:

Nope, it's erased and gone . . .

The note said something about how you were at least able to make confrontations and how I missed you and hugs. Mottttttttttttt

The sappy stuff isn't like him. It's his imitation of friendship, what he imagines he should say. But it's clear he's trying to say that things are all right again, so I don't call him on it. We spend the day writing back and forth. With the laptop, Mot is prolific. He writes about the things he's done since we last talked, and they're the same things he'd done in the days before he disappeared. He didn't try to fast in the desert or run off to Europe. He was doing Motley things, he says. *Same old same old.* He never says what drew him away or why he was able to come back. There are no clues in the anecdotes he sends.

I stepped outside and noted the Blood Mobile, ads said they'd be there and I wanted to give. I was the 1st customer. Sorry, they told me, my blood pressure was too high—150/100. Wouldn't taking blood lower it—they didn't know. I thought that was not excusable. You don't know?

By the end of the day, he's talking about Oklahoma City again, seemingly ready to move on as if nothing has happened.

It heals me in some small way to have Mot back. To have one person from this miserable year who says to me, "You are a help." One person who doesn't say, "Better not let me catch you in the parking lot alone."

I call the KOA outside Oklahoma City to be sure of the reservation and begin reading Websites about what to see and do while we're there. Mot suggests that I fly this time. "It's ridiculous," he says, his voice a little paternal, "for you to spend two days in the car each way. That must be torture!" He cobbles together a way for me to fly from Pittsburgh to OKC for less than three hundred dollars. It involves flying standby on a series of commuter flights and could take from one day to four. Mot is brilliant at travelling on next to no money and lots of time. But I don't want to fly. I need those days in the car, two up and two back, the meditative trance of a long-distance drive. Silence and purpose combined in the single, simple task of moving forward.

ALLIGATOR GAR

If I am not for myself, who will be for me?
If I am not for others, what am I?
And if not now, when?
—**Rabbi Hillel**

Two weeks after he reestablishes contact, Mot and I meet up in Oklahoma City. Cell phones help. Staying in contact while I drive has robbed the *Big Guys Upstairs* of the chance to make a muddle of time or to convince Mot that they have somehow waylaid me. But more importantly, we are doing a thing we have done before. Our rendezvous no longer seems unlikely to either of us. I call him as soon as I have the key in hand, and he pulls up in the old gray sedan as I finish making my bed.

His car is louder than it had been, banging and knocking in a way that makes me wish I'd met him in Amarillo instead of asking him to drive 250 miles east. Together, we unload his blanket and pillow, the coffeepot, hot plate, and computer, and an odd assortment of herbal cures he has brought along. He leaves almost everything else in the trunk. "No use bringing it all in, when I'll be living out of the car again in a week," he says. Once we have the coffeepot set up and brewing, Mot stands on the porch and throws his arms wide. "Give me a hug already. Sheesh! You're usually the touchy-feely one."

I move closer and Mot grabs me, pinning my arms against my sides in his enthusiasm. When he notices I'm not hugging back, he tucks his arms under mine and rests his head against my shoulder. He is a man of varying height, sometimes several inches taller than I am, sometimes a few shorter. I don't know if it's because he hunches in on himself when the Others are particularly troublesome or if the paralysis causes him to stoop over when he puts weight on his left side. Maybe it's a combination of both, or a trick of my own faulty senses. Resting against me now, he seems tiny. With his head under my chin, arms wrapped around me, hands clasped between my shoulder blades, I feel as though I'm holding a child. I put one hand on the back of his head, the other around his shoulders, and cradle him to me protectively. He smells of road dust and the sweet-scented soap from the bathroom dispensers at Walmart.

I feel Mot change in my arms. At first stiff, after a moment he goes limp. I struggle to hold him up. He sobs once, then buries his face in my hair and draws a deep breath. Finally, he pulls himself up to his full height and steps away, patting me on my head. "Good to see you, kid," he says in an unfamiliar baritone. I start to answer, but he smiles and, in a voice I recognize as his, says, "I need a shower. You okay here for a little bit on your own?"

I don't know how many Toms I've held in my arms: the child, the man, the laborer, and the wanderer? Each distinct, cycling through the brief embrace. I watch the one I know best—the one who calls himself Mot— limp toward the showers, towel over his shoulder and a dop kit tucked under his arm. There is a fragile beauty to old men, strong arms thinned to gracefulness, straight backs bent to gentle curves. Cockiness softened into dignity. I stand on the porch watching him until he disappears into the main building.

The KOA east of Oklahoma City is in a nicer neighborhood than the one in Amarillo. We're in Kabin 1 again, but here the view from the porch is of the pool, not a stockyard. A few gentle hills keep the sky a manageable size. The cabin is decorated with kitschy Americana, and the back window looks out over a wood of scrub pine and post oak. Midday swelters outside, but inside it's cool and dark.

We spend the first afternoon lazing around the camp. I'm still a little dazed from the road, and Mot seems more wary of me than he was in Amarillo. Conversation doesn't come as easily to us. Questions hang in the air that neither of us wants to ask. *What was it that made you think you had to cut off all contact? Why have you come, when you're only going to leave again and I'll be* in the same lousy shape as before you came? What are we doing here? Now that it's not such a miracle that we are here at all, these questions will have to be answered. But we aren't ready for them, and so we are quiet.

Instead of talking, we swim. I do long, lazy sets of laps while Mot mostly lies in the sun, jumping into the pool for a moment or two to cool down. I've chosen to arrive on a Monday in the hope that we'll have the campground mostly to ourselves, but it's crowded. We stay at the pool for about an hour, until a gaggle of young children arrive with rafts, squirt guns, and one frazzled mother trying to oversee the whole passel of them. Their games are too boisterous for us. I can't swim around their rafts, and Mot keeps getting caught in the crossfire of the squirt-gun battle. And I don't fully trust Mot—will never again fully trust Mot—around children. When it's clear that the mother isn't going to do anything to settle them down, we gather our things and walk back to the cabin.

Mot has spent the last few days scouting out the area near the campsite, but neither one of us knows anything about Oklahoma City proper except what we read in the article by Matt Gross. As I shower, Mot logs on to his laptop and plays around with Google Earth. He finds directions to the zoo, a theme park called Frontier City, and museums devoted to fine art, natural history, and cowboy culture. But these aren't the things we're looking for. So we set out with nothing but a tiny tourist-brochure map of the city and Mot's uncanny ability to find the nearest Walmart in any town.

Oklahoma City is clean, prosperous, the opposite of Amarillo. We find a Walmart, but satisfied with knowing where it is, we don't bother to go in. Instead, we backtrack to the neighborhood called Bricktown, a revitalized area. Driving around, we point out galleries we might like to see, but we don't actually stop until we come across the Bass Pro Shop.

Near the front of the store, fish swim in a wall-sized aquarium. We stop to watch. Two old men argue about a long, fearsome-toothed predator swimming lazily through the tank. "I tell you, it's an eel," says one to the other. "No, it ain't," says the second. "It's a fish. It's got fins, it can't be no eel."

Mot steps forward and says quietly, authoritatively, "It's an alligator gar." The other two old men turn to look at him. "They get big. The biggest one ever caught was over three hundred pounds. And they're mean. See that double row of teeth? They'll do real damage if you get too close. Live in the man-made lakes around the state; in fact, that's the only kind of lakes there are in Oklahoma. Did you know this is the only state without any natural lakes at all?"

The two old men stare. I stare. "Well, now, ain't that interesting," says the first, after a moment or two. "Where exactly are you from?" He peers at Mot, sizing him up.

"Pennsylvania," Mot says, and then he walks off toward the fishing boats.

"How did you know all of that?" I ask. Mot has said that this is his first time stopping in Oklahoma, and unlike in Amarillo, he doesn't name the trees for me or give me local history lessons.

"I told you, I'm a smart man," he says with a wink.

"Yes, I know you're a smart man, but you're no Okie, or much of a fisherman. So, how did you know all that?"

Mot laughs and then confesses. "There was a bulletin board with a picture of the fish and a poster some school kid had made about it beside the aquarium, but the rest of you couldn't see it because they had a display of fishing tackle blocking it from every angle but mine." He shrugs. "But, you know, I like to talk, and they seemed like nice enough old codgers. So what's the harm?"

I laugh and let him lead me into the boat showroom. He shows me the models he likes, the ones he doesn't. When he was a child, he says, his father kept a house and a fishing boat at the Jersey shore. "We weren't rich, but we weren't poor, either. We had nice stuff and lived in a nice neighborhood. We were part of the community, even a knucklehead like me."

His middle-classness is important to him and he insists on it even now that he has been homeless for thirty years. He'll admit that he's broke but never that he's poor.

Bored with the boats, I wander over to the camping gear. It's strange to stand among four-season tents and Arctic-rated sleeping bags with a homeless man. We wander through aisle after aisle of things that would make his life easier. But of course, if he could afford them, he could afford a place to live and wouldn't need them. I finger forty-dollar quick-drying long johns while Mot moons over a front-and-backpack that runs almost two hundred dollars. "I could carry twice as much with one of those," he says.

I pull it down and hand it to him. "Try it on."

"No. I mean, I've had a design like this in mind for years. I'd rather build it myself. This one isn't as well designed as the one I came up with, anyway." He pushes my hand back toward the rack. "Put it back. I mean, do you really think a broken guy like me could carry as much as that would hold?"

"Maybe you could carry more if you had the weight distributed evenly," I say.

Mot pats his book bag—all he carries, even when he doesn't have a car. "Nope, these days, if it won't fit in here, it's too much for me to haul around. A man has to travel light."

I don't know if he really thinks he couldn't carry the pack, or if he's afraid I'll offer to buy it for him. Money doesn't flow easily between us. Before both trips, my mother gave me a few hundred dollars, and both times I've split it with him so that he, too, would have some walking around money. This doesn't bother Mot. He doesn't know my mother, but it makes some kind of sense to him that she would send me with a gift. However, Mot won't take money directly from me. He will allow me to pay for things only if they are for both of us: the cabin, a dinner out, groceries. But he won't let me buy anything for him alone. I've offered tents, new shoes, prepaid gasoline cards, and now this pack. He's turned down every offer I've made. In truth, I'm grateful. There is so much he needs. If he were willing to let me pay, how would I know when to stop? How could I not rent him an apartment, make sure he had heat, try to keep him fed and in the medicines he needs but doesn't have?

It takes hours, but finally we tire of looking at fish, boats, and expensive ways to make living out of doors an adventure rather than a hardship. As we leave, Mot makes a wrong turn and finds himself pushing against a turnstile that will not give. It's an entrance; the exit is to the right. I motion for him to join me, but he shakes his head and contorts his body around the immovable gate. It takes several seconds, and the arms of the turnstile gouge into his stomach and back, but eventually he squeezes through. I go around the right way and we meet up in the parking lot.

This isn't the first time I've seen Mot set out to do a thing one way, discover it's the wrong way, and be unable to change directions. He seems to find great danger in admitting mistakes; I don't know if it's a leftover fear of punishment or a strategy for keeping the *Big Guys Upstairs* from stopping him from doing a thing once he has set his mind to it. But I've learned not to try to sway him once his course is set. Instead, I smile at the people who stare and shake my head *no* to stop the greeter who walks toward Mot, clearly intending to point him in the right direction. If I can't change Mot, then maybe I can change the world around him, at least in little ways. I smile at the people who stare at us, nod in agreement when he says something outlandish to a stranger. My middle-aged, middle-class ordinariness does, sometimes, make the difference. Because I'm the sort of person you expect to see at a Walmart or a bookstore or a restaurant, some of his unexpectedness is camouflaged. People still stare, but not for as long, and we are never asked to leave. When he's alone, he has told me, he is often chased away.

It's late, and we didn't bother to get directions to the *pho* restaurants before leaving the campground, so we agree on pizza. Neither of us will eat the yeasty-doughed, bland pies that could be delivered to the campsite in thirty minutes or less, but we'd seen a place called Falcone's, not far from the Bass Pro Shop, that looked promising.

Mot often says that when he was still a working man, he lived on pizza, beer, and little else. That's hard to imagine, since he sets out to find the health food store in each new town after finding the Walmart and before looking for the library. But he had hard, physical jobs when he worked: construction, bricklaying, and day labor. The sorts of job a transient person can pick up and walk away from easily. He says it kept him fit. Now, he allows himself pizza only once or twice a month. The rest of the time he lives off canned vegetables eaten cold, dried fruits, and instant oatmeal made surreptitiously at restaurants with self-serve hot water for tea. Having rationed pizza, he has grown picky. We are both steadfast believers in the superiority of New York–style pizza.

Falcone's could be in Brooklyn. The air is redolent with garlic, and the pies—large and flat-crusted—are sold whole or by the slice. We stand at the counter and it feels like a feast day, a celebration. Mot gives me a sidelong look, as if to be certain he's not being too extravagant, and then orders a large pie with mushrooms, onions, and olives. While it's being made, we run to a nearby liquor store and pick up a six-pack of beer. Somehow, these simple tasks bring us back together. The questions that have been hovering over us all day evaporate. We've remembered how to enjoy each other's company and let go of the things we can't change.

Pizza and beer in hand, we return to the cabin. Mot spreads a towel down on my bed and gets the camp plates from the gear I've brought. I use the trash can to ice the beer. When the picnic is all laid out, Mot pulls out his laptop.

"I've got a movie," he says, smiling. I'm surprised and pleased at this. "I found a copy of Jean Rouch's *Les Maîtres Fous* on YouTube and downloaded it. The version I found isn't great. It's grainy and has subtitles, but you'll see what I mean about the whole thing." He sets the laptop up at the end of the bed and settles into his camp chair.

One of the first things Mot told me about himself was that he'd gotten an A in a narrative film class he'd taken at the University of Vermont, in spite of living outdoors and having to move around while he was in school. "College is something I always wanted to do. Sure, now I'll probably never finish it, because the *Big Guys Upstairs* don't want me to know anything, but at least I got through a couple of semesters. And for someone like me, that's really an accomplishment," he had said that first day, sitting beside my desk.

The film itself is hard to watch. Rouch recorded the rituals of a short-lived African sect known as the *Hauka*. Supplicants chew coca leaves so that they may become possessed by the spirits of the Dutch imperialists who had become their "masters." Possessed, they burn themselves, break taboo by eating a dog, and beat one another brutally. Still, it's a ceremony of empowerment—the oppressed become, for a while, the oppressors. Made in 1954, *Les Maîtres Fous* has always shocked its audiences, but I'm afraid to show my own disgust. How much of himself does Mot see in the grimacing faces of the Mad Masters?

While we watch, he points out film-student details: shot composition, editing choices, translation issues. He talks knowledgeably about the question of cultural imperialism and the African response to Rouch's filmmaking. But Mot never personalizes his commentary, he never says—as he did after we saw *Mr. Brooks*—this is just like me. Instead, he lectures me on the issues of colonialism and documentary film. It sounds as if he has memorized parts of a textbook, and maybe he has. A gift of his eidetic memory, the part of himself he calls the *Know-It-All*. I want to ask him if he sees himself in the film, but I don't. I'm not sure if it would be safe to make the connection if he has not.

After the film, I clean up while Mot goes out to tinker with his car in the cool of twilight. His side of the room is littered with crumpled drawings that seem to be plans for a trailer he could haul behind the sedan and the coils of aquarium tubing he always carries in his pockets. I've asked him what they're for, but he won't say. Perhaps he's afraid I will steal his next invention. While I straighten up the cabin, Mot drains the radiator of his car. Tomorrow he wants to add a silicon sealant that he believes will fix the engine, and it has to be dry first. I don't even pretend to understand, but I hope it works. The sedan doesn't look like it will ever be drivable again.

INSTANT PHO

It is said that if you know your enemies and know yourself,
you will not be imperiled in a hundred battles; if you do not
know your enemies but do know yourself, you will win one
and lose one; if you do not know your enemies nor yourself,
you will be imperiled in every single battle.

—Sun Tzu

On our second day in Oklahoma City, Mot and I
wake up early to swim before the families take over the pool. His com-
promised left side makes swimming difficult. He tires quickly and can't
manage a straight line in the lap lane. But it's nice to be in the water, cool
in the already sweltering morning heat. So he pulls himself along the edge
of the pool, coaching.

"You should kick more with your legs," he calls out when I do my un-
trained version of the breaststroke. "Lift your head further out of the water. You glide too much; you're never going to lose any weight doing it that
way." I switch to the crawl. "You splash too much," he says, "and you look
like a drowning cow. What are you doing, the dog paddle?"

Our friendship dampens the insults. He can say things to me that
would make me furious if they came from anyone else, even my husband.
Particularly my husband. But although the things he says don't really hurt
my feelings, at least not after I remind myself that Mot isn't trying to be
unkind and that this is his version of affectionate teasing, they do worry
me. They are cracks in the wall we've built between us and the *Big Guys Up-*

stairs. Mot knows when he is being unkind, and he seems less able to stop himself than he was in Morgantown or Amarillo.

Still, we are good company for each other. Maybe the insults are tests, or maybe they are artifacts of a life lived mostly away from social niceties. The important thing is that they do not matter enough to make either of us lose sight of the fact that we enjoy one another. But I'm tired from the drive and a little annoyed by the crowded noisiness of the campground, and the snide remarks rankle. I have to work to maintain my good cheer. When I get tired of swimming laps, I float on my back, eyes closed against the sun. Mot sneaks up beside me and grabs me round the waist.

"The thing about being in the pool," he says, "is that it's like being on the moon . . . everybody is Superman." He picks me up and tosses me a few feet away, into the deep end. I come up laughing and find him looking at me quizzically. "You know, that was something different," he says, and I nod.

"Different is good," I say, but it's a question.

"Different is the only choice I've got," he answers.

I don't know how to understand what has just happened. I'm not sure if it was childish horseplay or something else. There was an aggressiveness in the way he grabbed me. I'm not afraid that it was sexual—the look on his face suggested victory, not seduction—but it leaves me wary and uncomfortable. For the rest of our time at the pool, I'm afraid to let him out of my sight. I'm not certain if this new strangeness is about me or only happens to coincide with my visit, but it feels ominous.

After about an hour, when the pool once again becomes the property of screaming children cannonballing off the sides and fighting with water pistols, we walk back to the cabin. I stay two paces behind, unwilling to close the distance between us. I sit on the porch swing and pile the wet towels on it so there isn't room for Mot to join me. He stays in the yard, checking the engine of the sedan to be certain it's drained before he pours the sealant in.

"That should do it, but it's got to set for twenty-four hours. See?" he says, showing me the directions on the bottle as if I might argue. "I need to get some more sealant for my car at Pep Boys and a couple of fuel and oil additives for the Toyota. Your car needs some serious help, too. I mean, look at it!"

"What's wrong with my car?" I ask. I'd had it checked out before the long drive and my mechanic had said everything was fine.

"I don't know, but you can tell by looking at it that something is." He shakes his head. "That demon symbol on the front, to start with. Any car with that thing on it can't be good. I mean, I admit it's in better shape than mine, but couldn't you have bought an American car?"

The Toyota logo on my car could, now that he points it out, look like an abstraction of a bull's head inside an oval. I'd never given it much thought, but a man with *Moloch* in his throat would see it. *Moloch*, the god with a man's body and a bull's head, the god of the golden calf. Now that I see it, I'm surprised Mot will get into my car at all. But he does.

This time, before we leave, we download directions to a *pho* restaurant. We have asked the campground manager to recommend one, but although he lives in Oklahoma City, he doesn't know what we are talking about. This makes me sad and reaffirms Mot's sense that eating Vietnamese food is un-American. While Mot digs around in the trunk of his car, I sit on the porch swing reading him reviews of the different noodle houses.

"Here's one," I say, reading from the Website *Pho Fever*. "Pho Hoa. It's on Northwest 23 Street. One reviewer calls it the gold standard for *pho* in Oklahoma City. Another person says it's the best in an area with four or five other *pho* places." I show the reviews to Mot. "Besides, it's on a numbered street, so we'll have a better chance of finding it."

"I know I said we could go there, but I'm having second thoughts," Mot says. I am using MapQuest to find a Pep Boys near the area known as "Little Saigon" but not having much luck. "I'll try, but I don't think Fahey would like it. The last time I went into a Vietnamese restaurant it didn't go very well. I mean, I was trying to be nice, but then they started talking to me, and I thought, 'Fahey wouldn't like this at all, me being chummy with the 'mese.'"

He pronounces it "meese," and for a second I think he's making a mouse joke.

"I mean, what, you get to fight a war with us, kill a bunch of our guys, and then we're supposed to act like nothing happened? So I guess I got a little excited and maybe a little loud. They wouldn't serve me, and they made me leave." He gives me a sheepish look. "I mean, I know that's not a likable thing to do, but you gotta stand by your friends, right?"

Fahey, one of the few people from his past Mot talks about, and the only one other than his sister that he calls by name, is another mentally ill veteran. At one time, he and Mot seem to have been traveling buddies.

"Before I met him, Fahey had a family and everything. But he was a drunk, and his family kicked him out. So he didn't have anyone but an old bleep-up like me to buddy around with. We'd set up camp together and I'd buy the beer. But finally he dried out, at least enough for his family to let him come home. So that was that. I didn't see him any after that."

He doesn't seem to hold a grudge, though, or to think that Fahey might have reached out to help Mot once he himself was back on his feet. Mot doesn't expect much from the rest of us. He's happy as long as we aren't trying to kill him, but he mostly thinks we are.

In the end, we settle on going straight to the nearby Pep Boys and then seeing where the day takes us. Mot wants another bottle of the sealant and some WD-40. "It's shameful how dirty your engine is," he tells me, propping up the hood to see if he can figure out what's "wrong" before I drive the car home. "I mean, I know you just drove a little over a thousand miles, but this hasn't been cleaned in a long time. You told me you took the car to your mechanic before you made the trip." He looks at me as if the dirty engine is proof that I'm lying to him. "Well, did you?"

"Yes, I took the car to the mechanic. He changed the oil, checked all the fluids and the tire pressure, that kind of thing."

"But he didn't clean the engine?" Mot asks, exasperated.

"I don't know. I didn't look, and I didn't ask. Isn't that why I have a mechanic, so I don't have to worry about such things?"

Mot lets out a deep sigh. "This is why women always get ripped off by mechanics." He looks at me and shakes his head in disappointment. "I thought you were different. Can't be like that, you know. They'll take advantage of you if you let them see you're just a girl."

I want to protest, to do a brief version of my perfectly-capable-of-taking-care-of-myself speech, but there are too many layers here. Like his odd moments of racism, Mot's sexism is tied more to the rantings of the Big Guys Upstairs than to prejudice. His travels have left him a little horrified by how the United States looks from outside its borders. He says his life has taught him to be grateful that he was born white and male. But the Big Guys Upstairs are always calling him a stupid Polack and threatening to turn him into a girl. Sometimes their small-minded ways bleed over into who he is, no matter how much he fights them.

Besides, my engine is filthy and mechanics have been ripping me off for years. Mot knows that I once paid five hundred dollars for a rebuilt alternator and that I burned up the engine of my last car because I thought I could drive another twenty miles before stopping to find out why the check-oil light had come on. So I tell him he's right and give him the keys.

Oklahoma City should be easy to navigate. It's a grid, more or less, with roads running not only on the cardinal directions but also southeast and southwest, northeast and northwest. Scotti has mounted a compass on my dashboard, and within the first half hour Mot and I realize that something's wrong with it. Using it to navigate, we find ourselves in the southeastern corner of the city when we'd been trying to go southwest. Later, we'll check it against a compass Mot keeps in his glove box and find that mine is somehow misaligned by almost fifteen degrees.

We are happy to be lost. It gives some shape to the day because now we know that our task for the afternoon is to slowly make our way back to the KOA. We stop anytime something catches our attention. This is a new city for both of us, and we're content to watch it go slowly by outside the windows while we talk and drink gas-station coffee.

We drive mostly through residential neighborhoods. The houses are low, new, and clean. It isn't until we drive past the Oklahoma National Memorial and Museum that I remember that until 9/11, Oklahoma City was the synecdoche for terrorism in this country.

"I forgot about the bombing here," I say. "I can't believe I forgot that, but I did."

"You forgot?" Mot sounds almost angry. "I don't believe you. It must be a trick. *Moloch* and *Dubja* must have made you forget, or tricked you into bringing me here. I mean, *They* are always trying to drag me to places where lots of people died, so those people can glom on to me, use my resources so they don't have to be dead."

I'm horrified by my carelessness. This could be the breaking point for our friendship if one of us doesn't figure a way out of the narrative his illness is starting to build—the one in which I have tricked him into coming to Oklahoma City to carry these new souls around with his aunts and the *Harpies.*

"It must be hard to believe, but I genuinely didn't remember. Let's just get out of here as fast as we can and not come back to this part of town." I squeal away from the stoplight.

"I don't know. *They* could be pulling your strings and you might not even know it. I mean, sure, you're a girl who knows how to take a punch, and you can make a confrontation when you know what we're up against, but that doesn't mean you can't be tricked." Mot shakes his head. "Look at me. I walked around like this for fifty-some years and had no idea what was going on up here." He motions upward with his thumb again.

I speed through downtown Oklahoma City. "Let's just get away as fast as we can," I mutter.

Mot is silent as I navigate back to the campground. When I ask him which way he thinks we should go, he only shrugs. Eventually, I end up on the Stanley Draper Expressway, a part of Highway 40 I remember from my drive through Oklahoma City on my way to Amarillo, but we're going the wrong way. I find an exit, turn around, and start the drive back to the campground.

"I don't want to go back yet," Mot says. "I mean, either the damage is done and all those souls got their hooks in me, or we got away in time. No way to tell until I go to sleep tonight. Might be my last day. Better enjoy it. Let's go see if we can find that damned noodle restaurant you've been yammering about."

Maybe we have escaped disaster; maybe we've only postponed it. Like Mot says, we'll just have to wait and see. Delusion is a malleable thing, reworking itself to incorporate each new event in Mot's life. I can try to avoid being woven into the narrative of his persecution, but I expect that ultimately I will fail. This is a friendship to make the most of while it lasts, not to count on for the long run.

"You know," Mot says when the silence has gone on longer than he can allow, "I used to just walk around like a total lunkhead. I had no idea what was going on, but I wanted to fit in, to find my niche. And Brunhilda, the woman who took care of us while our mother was away, she was always trying to insinuate that I was gay. I think it's because she had a gay brother who sometimes came to visit us, and she wanted him to have someone to hang out with. Not like she was trying to fix us up or anything, just that she thought we were alike. I'd be watching those old shows like *American Bandstand* and she'd ask me which girls I liked. You know, which ones I'd be interested in. And no matter which one I'd pick, she'd say, 'Yeah, I think my brother would like that one, too.' And we all knew he was gay, so I figure she was trying to say that I was gay, too, or maybe convince me to be gay so her brother would have somebody. I dunno." He watches me, maybe looking for some sign of shock or disbelief. I'm not shocked, and I believe that at least the kernel of this story is true, that he did watch *American Bandstand* with the housekeeper. I don't know this story, but I know enough of his other ones to understand it.

"So, anyway, I always thought maybe it worked, you know, maybe I was gay. I mean, I didn't *want* to be gay, but things sure weren't working out for me on the other front. I mean, what girl wants a guy with all this stuff wrong with him, right?" He looks at me again, and this time I smile, trying to soften the fact that I, too, can't imagine any girl, or any man either, wanting a guy like him. He chuckles and goes on, "So, you know, when I was younger, there used to be this one corner where all the gays hung out. Everyone knew it, but nobody bothered them because, well, it was their corner. So one day I got really loaded and I figured, 'What the hell, I guess I'm supposed to be gay.' I went over to their corner. I walked up and just said out loud, 'I guess I'm one of you cocksucking faggots now. I don't want to be, but I guess I am. So now what?' And, of course, they all just looked at me like I was crazy and walked away." Mot laughs. "I mean, sure, now I know what an idiot thing that was to say. But back then, I was just looking for someplace to belong. It's hard, you know, when nobody wants you. Not even the faggots." He laughs again, but it's a dry laugh, mirthless. "There you have it. The story of my life. No place to go, nobody to talk to." He leans over and puts a hand on my shoulder. "That's what's good about you. I can talk to you." He pets me the way one might pet a small child. "You're kind of a knucklehead, but at least we can have a conversation without you walking away."

His story breaks my heart, but I laugh along with him and pat the hand that is patting my shoulder. "That's a tough break," I say as cheerfully as I can manage. "I mean, here you are finally giving in just so you can belong to a group, a community, and what happens?"

"Well, yeah, but I get their point. I mean, not only do you have to wonder who'd want this nutcase around, but it wasn't a very nice thing to say.

But I didn't know any better back then. I mean, we called 'em cocksucking faggots, so I figured that was what they called themselves. I was a zombie for my first fifty years, you know."

"I know," I say, and then, too sad for another story, I point to a sign for a Vietnamese grocery store. "Let's go in there. I love shopping in international groceries, and maybe we can buy the stuff to make pho at the cabin and not have to go to a restaurant at all." It's generous that Mot has offered to go with me to the noodle restaurant, but I don't want pho badly enough to risk the meltdown he's predicting. As he says, *There's something over here that doesn't want us to get clobbered without a warning.*

"Okay," Mot says hesitantly. "I'll do my best. But if I say we gotta leave, we better leave. I don't know if I can keep my mouth shut. Only thing to do is try, I guess."

The store is huge and smells of lemongrass, pepper, anise, and fresh mango. Mot has been in search of lemongrass to make a tea—he read somewhere that it would be good for his blood pressure—and when he finds whole bunches of it in the produce aisle, he completely abandons his misgivings and gives himself over to the charm of the place. We hand each other unfamiliar things: galangal root, lychee nuts, tamarind pulp, and fresh wood ears. Everything that catches our eye goes into the cart. On the shelves, I find candied olives and plastic bowls of instant pho. Mot picks out three different kinds of hot sauce. We buy bottles of aloe vera juice with floating chunks of cactus and overpriced candied ginger in a pretty tin.

We push our cart full of the most improbable things we could find to the line at the single register in the front of the store. The checkout girl smiles at Mot and holds up the candied olives. "Oh, very good," she says, laughing and nodding. "Not many Americans eat." Then she asks, "You were in Vietnam, in the service, so you eat these?" I hold my breath, but Mot only shakes his head.

"Nope," he says. "This is her stuff, mostly. I don't think she can make a meal of it, but she can probably cook up a pretty scary science project."

Once we've loaded the groceries into the car, Mot turns to me and says, "Okay, that wasn't so bad, but I definitely can't go back. Did you hear those people talking about me?" He holds his hand out for the keys.

"What people? I didn't hear anyone but the girl at the counter speaking English." I let him drive, hoping it will center him.

"That's the whole problem," he says. "I mean, I know it's me. I can't go into Mexican restaurants, either, because when they're all talking and I can't understand what they're saying, I know it has to be about me." He takes the keys from me and gets into the driver's side. "But what I don't know is if I'm being paranoid or if the Jesuses have really made me able to understand all these other languages, at least on some level. And don't tell me you know, because you don't. It's happened sometimes; people will be talking in a language I've never heard before and suddenly I'll understand everything they're saying and we'll be able to have a conversation." He motions upward with his thumb. "That's when the *Know-It-All* is here. When it's here I know everything, but when it's gone it takes all of that knowledge with it and leaves me in the dark again. Sometimes *They* say I should send the *Know-It-All* to you. Like a gift. That it's the one good thing we could give you. But it isn't easy to live with, let me tell you. It wouldn't be a very good gift at all." He smiles at me. "Besides, you already think you know more than you do. It wouldn't be good for you to know even more." He pats my shoulder again, as if to say that it's okay, he likes me anyway.

Mot drives to a liquor store we'd passed on the way into town to buy a bottle of rum to go with our aloe juice and coconut water. The man at the counter is Asian, and Mot decides he'd better wait outside while I pay.

"I don't think we should push it," he says. "I've been good all day, but you never know when I'm going to start acting like a nut. So you pay and I'll wait by the car." With the bottle in hand, we decide Pep Boys can wait until tomorrow, and we drive back to camp.

Mot's moments of insight, his being able to say *you never know when I'm going to start acting like a nut* and *I know that wasn't a likable thing to say*, make it possible for me to look past the racism and homophobia in what he says. In fact, I think the world would be a better place if more of us had his capacity for self-awareness. Still, it gets tiring.

"I've had all the adventure I can take for one day," I say.

"Then it's a good thing you don't live in here," Mot says and rolls his eyes. "The adventure never stops, although it's more like a nightmare. Every time I think things are quieting down or that maybe I'm winning, they just switch the program on me." He sighs. "I don't think they're going to let you hang out much longer. I don't know what they're going to do, but if I were you, I'd keep on my toes. Lot of bad guys over here, like I said."

"I'm going to go take another shower." I need a few minutes to myself. His warnings are starting to worry me. They're more frequent and ominous than they've ever been before. But I don't know which one of us might get hurt, and I'm convinced that abandoning him would be wrong in a way I wouldn't be able to live with. "Why don't you look through the stuff we bought and see what we're going to have for dinner."

I stand under the drizzle of hot water for longer than I need to, wondering if we're going to make it through this trip. As we grow more familiar, it seems we also grow farther apart. I think back to his email. *The great difference is partnership and newness.* Both seem to be wearing thin.

We spend our last two days at the cabin, eating the oddities from the Vietnamese grocery and ice cream sandwiches from the camp store. There is a Center for Native American Culture nearby, and Mot has talked about going there to consult with a shaman.

"Maybe they'd know what to do with this mess up here," he says, handing me the brochure for a third, then a fourth time.

"Maybe," I say noncommittally, and then I distract him with the list of other things we intend to do around camp that afternoon. I don't have it in me to spring Mot on some poor, unsuspecting tour guide who he thinks might know a mystical cure to rid him of the *Others*. I can inflict his just-to-the-left-of-things ways on waitresses and campground attendants, but my sense of decorum will not stretch far enough for what he has in mind.

It rains most of these last two days, so instead of looking for adventure we laze around the cabin. I knit while Mot draws a new set of plans for his front-and-backpack. He searches Google Books until he finds a Max Brand western that sounds good to him, and we take turns reading chapters to one another. The story is expected, but it's pleasant to be read to. It revolves around a young man who is abandoned by his family and so has to make his own way in the rough-and-tumble frontier. If Mot draws any parallels to his own life, he doesn't voice them.

On the last evening, the weather clears and we walk the short trail that runs behind the cabins and RV campsites. I'm astounded by the RVs, which are huge and new and, I imagine, ridiculously expensive. There is something awful about knowing that so many of our campground neighbors have an extra home they drive to vacations while Mot has none. At least there is something awful about it to me. It doesn't bother Mot at all.

"So many families," Mot says as we walk past another cluster of grandparents, parents, and children finishing up dinner around a campfire. "That's how it's supposed to be, but not for knuckleheads like you and me. We're stuck with each other."

But of course, I have family, nuclear and extended. Both have made room for Mot, have at least given me the freedom to make these trips, but I am not, like him, untethered and alone in the world. I wonder if I've been dishonest, made him think that this untetheredness, this singularity, is something we share when really my life is more like the lives of these vacationing families than it is like his. Have I let him believe we're in this together when I'm only visiting his difficult life, not living it with him?

We stop along a ridge to watch the sun set.

"You know, kid," Mot says, "I think maybe things will get better. I mean, you're kind of a nut, but you know how to make a confrontation and you don't back down when the Others try to scare you." He points to a place on the horizon where we can barely make out buzzards circling over an unseen carcass. "Most of the time, that would scare the hell out of me. I'd be sure that those birds were looking for me. But with you here, I'm pretty sure they aren't. I mean, you seem to think I'm alive, so maybe I am."

This proclamation is as frightening as it is encouraging. Tonight is our last night in Oklahoma City, and we don't have a plan to see one another again. My job at Friendship Room is over, and with it, the weeks of vacation time I'd used for my two trips. When I get back to Morgantown, I'll be returning to school, and without a job, I won't have the money for these trips. I'm afraid that perhaps I have made Mot trust me right when I'm going to have to desert him.

"What are you going to do when I leave?" I ask.

"Probably head on up the road a ways. Amarillo was perfect," he says, "but not this place. Once you're gone, they're sure to find some reason to run me out of town or put me in jail." And it's true that in Amarillo Mot faded into the falling-apartness of things, but here he stands out against the prosperity.

"Do you want to come back to Morgantown with me?" I know the answer but don't feel that relieves me of the obligation to make the offer.

"No way! Are you nuts?" Mot shakes his head and laughs. "I don't think you should go back, either." I start to answer him, but he puts a hand up to stop me. "I mean, I know you're going to go back. There's no talking you out of a thing once you've set your mind to it, even if you're wrong. But really, I think we should both go fast in the desert and see if we can't get ourselves sane."

I understand this to be his way of saying he'll miss me.

"I think you're right that you probably shouldn't stay here," I say. "Not really our sort of town. Why don't we leave together in the morning, and I'll follow you until you find a town you think you'd like to stay in for a while? That way, if the car breaks down, you won't be stranded."

I get Mot to agree to drive a little farther east, where I'd stopped for gas in towns with abandoned buildings and rusted trailers instead of the shopping malls and large new homes that surround us here. I would like to get him out of Oklahoma altogether because those towns had looked too small for him to be able to fade into an existing community of homeless men, and the desert seems a dangerous place to live out of doors. But he can't agree to go far enough to leave Oklahoma behind.

"We'll just have to start out and see where we end up," Mot says, and then he gathers the things he needs to put a final bottle of sealant into his sedan. "Let me see what I can do with this hunk of junk tonight. Should be okay, but I guess it can't hurt to have you around for backup." I gather the laundry and set off to call Scotti to tell him I may be home a day or so later than I'd planned.

Scotti and I have barely spoken since I left Morgantown for this trip. He's preoccupied with Rita, whose nephews are visiting, and this preoccupation has become a serious point of contention between us. She called one evening before I left, and I could hear the boys—who are between eleven and fourteen—crying in the background. When I told her that Scotti wasn't at home, she screamed into the phone, *You tell him he better get here quick or I am going to kill these fucking children and then myself! You tell him that he has to get out here right now and take these fucking brats back to their parents or I will beat their fucking brains out!*

I was stunned. Since marrying Scotti, I have seen sides of Rita she was able to keep hidden from me during our years of friendship. Scotti often counsels her from our home phone, and our house is too small for me not to overhear. But he has always said what a fabulous aunt she is, how she is the most loving and stable person in her nephews' lives. Scotti is, in fact, the one who picks the boys up in their hometown an hour and a half away to bring them to her because he says it is so good for all of them.

On the rare occasions we have talked during this trip, it has been to argue about this. What I heard on the phone was not good for those boys, and nothing he has said has convinced me otherwise. And so we have the same conversation every time I call. I'm not convinced that I don't have an obligation to call Child Protective Services. He insists that what I heard was protected by privilege.

"But I'm not her therapist," I say.

"But I am, and she called here looking for me."

"But you're not, really. I mean, you don't get paid to treat her, and you're not currently licensed."

"I am her therapist and I'm not having this conversation with you again." But we do have the conversation again, and we will have some variation of it off and on for the next several years.

Mot tinkers with his car well into the night while I pack up the cabin. He's happiest, most centered, when he's working. Back when he was in Morgantown, he had come to Friendship Room one Saturday with a list: two new mop heads, four bottles of Murphy's Oil Soap, and a large package of steel wool. "If you'll go out and get all this," he had said, "I'll fix these floors for you." The wooden floors, which might once have been beautiful, were dark with grime and coffee stains. I didn't think he could do much without a buffer or a sander, but touched by the fact that he wanted to make the effort, I left the program assistant in charge of the room and went to the store.

Mot and I stayed for three hours after closing time moving furniture, scrubbing at old stains with the steel wool, and washing the floors with bucket after bucket of diluted Murphy's Oil Soap. While we worked, he pointed out other things he would like to fix. A busted lamp. An easy chair with a missing leg, propped up with a small stack of books. A cabinet door that had come off its hinges. He made lists of the things he'd need, and over the next few weeks I brought tools from Scotti's workshop so that he could work on these projects. By the time he left, every broken thing at Friendship Room had been fixed or discarded as beyond repair. The room was less shabby, though I may have been the only person who noticed.

MOT BREAKS DOWN

You can't see anything from a car; you've got to get out
of the goddamn contraption and walk, better yet crawl,
on hands and knees, over the sandstone and through
the thornbrush and cactus. When traces of blood begin
to mark your trail, you'll see something, maybe.
—**Edward Abbey**

I'm a believer in early starts. By 6:00 a.m. on the day
we're to leave, I'm ready to hit the road, but Mot's still sleeping that odd,
dead sleep of his, never moving, his breath as shallow as a baby's.

Mot's car has gone from bad to worse while we've been at the KOA. It
overheated on the one short trip we made to town in it, although he as-
sures me that it will be fine on the highway and that last night he was able
take care of the coolant leak. We've spent a lot of this trip at Pep Boys buying additives, gauges, and widgety things, and he's been pouring silicon
leak-fixing goo into the engine all week. When I say that I think the engine
block is cracked, he fixes me with a warning glare and says, "No, that can't
be what's wrong, because that's something I couldn't fix," so I let it go.

He has also been trying to convince me that I need a summer thermostat for my car, and to let him under my hood so he can install one.
I've called my mechanic back home, who said he's never heard of such a
thing and to leave well enough alone. Mot showed me one at Pep Boys, so
I know they exist. My faith in my mechanic is a little damaged. How can he
not have heard of a part that's right there on the shelf in front of me? Still,

the slow demise of the old gray sedan isn't a testament to Mot's skills, either, so I haven't agreed.

Our goal for today is to reach Henryetta and settle Mot in so he can get serious about fixing up the car. We've checked online, and the city has a Walmart and a couple of auto parts stores. Really, though, the important thing is that it's farther east than Prague. Mot has promised to make a slow journey back to my part of the country, but the whole thing could come derailed if he broke down there. Prague, Oklahoma, is home to the National Shrine of the Infant Jesus of Prague. There are billboards for it along Highway 40, and even driving past them seems risky.

"The Bible tells you how to make a Jesus," Mot has explained to me. "I mean, the lineage is all right there, all you have to do is re-create it." He believes Jesuses can be bred. But in his strange theology, they are more often made. "It happens all the time. People need a savior, so they pick out some poor kid and make him the Jesus for their community. All you have to do is break a baby, break his body. Then that kid has to take on the sins of anyone who asks to be saved. That's how it works with a Jesus; you can't pick and choose. If someone asks, you have to save them. So the kid they turn into a Jesus never has a chance. I mean, sure, some kids might think it was a good thing, but what do they know at that age?"

I don't believe Mot could survive breaking down near the shrine. I think that whatever he would become there would make the Mot from the Amarillo Walmart parking lot seem like he was doing fine. So when he still isn't up at eight, I bring badly brewed cups of coffee from the camp store back to the cabin and wake him. I need to get him east of the Infant of Prague no matter what happens, and that means it's time to go.

The plan is for Mot to set the pace and for me to follow. He says his car does best if he doesn't go over forty-five miles per hour. We each have a cell phone, but he doesn't think he can answer his while driving, so we set up an elaborate language of signals. If I see smoke coming from his tailpipe, I'm to turn on my emergency flashers. If he turns on his, it means his car's running hot and he needs to pull over. Two short blasts of a horn means *Do you want to stop at the next exit?* An answer of one honk means *no*, two *yes*. And so on.

We make it less than ten miles before his car overheats for the first time, outside Midwest City. We stop and Mot pops open the hood on the off-ramp. He measures fluids and adds coolant and oil. He had topped them both off before we left.

"Should we turn around?" I ask, pretty sure the answer is *yes*, even when he says *no*.

He thinks that the latest batch of silicon hasn't had a chance to work, or that maybe we'll have to stop at the next town and buy another bottle. I don't think so, but I keep quiet. Part of what I'm learning is how to go along.

The car dies two more times in the twenty-four miles between Midwest City and Dale. There, we pull into a gas station that seems to be the only inhabited building in the town. There is the shell of an old restaurant across the parking lot and the weathered foundation of a building that a faded billboard claims will one day be a casino. That's all. Just that, and desert.

Mot begins running water through the engine of the old sedan from a hose hooked to a spigot behind the gas station. I'm surprised that water is free in the desert. The thing steams and sputters for a good ten minutes as gallon after gallon pours out onto the hot, tarry blacktop. Still, Mot thinks the car can be saved.

The man in the gas station tells us that the nearest auto parts store is in Shawnee, a little less than ten miles away, and shows us on our map how to get there on the back roads. He comes outside to look at the car. "Park her around the back, in case you don't come back for her," he tells us.

Mot tries to explain what he thinks is wrong, but the man shakes his head. "Buddy, if this were my car, I'd have left it by the side of the road a long time ago. Don't look like it's worth pouring any more money into to me."

So we move the car to a spot between the rusted shell of an old VW Rabbit and the bedless frame of a pickup truck. Like the cattle skulls in cowboy movies, they mark the journeys of people who have tried, and failed, the same road we're traveling.

At the auto parts store in Shawnee, Mot and the kid behind the counter talk about the car for a long time in a language I only vaguely understand. I know the names of the parts, but not the parts themselves. Is a new water pump an easy fix, or something that will take a week and several hundred dollars? I have no frame of reference, but I'm with the gas station guy. I don't think the car is worth any more time or energy. When it looks like maybe the kid has talked Mot into a pile of parts and the conversation turns to taking the entire engine apart, I step in and point out that he has no place to work on the car and that he can't drive it this far or fix it where it's parked in Dale. There is no protection at all there from the harsh desert sun, no Walmart, no auto parts store.

The kid, though, must work on commission. He doesn't even acknowledge me, except to say to Mot, "Women! What do they know about a guy and his car, right?" Then he goes right back to trying to sell him the tools to install the new water pump.

"This is a four-hundred dollar car with mismatched doors and, most likely, a cracked engine block." I may not know much, but even I know that a cracked engine block is car cancer, terminal and swift. "Do you really think it's worth fixing?" I ask the kid pointedly.

"Well, sure," he says. "Any car's worth fixing, if it's the only car you've got."

This logic will work on Mot. I have to cut it off quickly. "Let me put it this way. If it was your car and you had to choose between staying here, isolated and homeless, or leaving it behind and going on down the road with a friend who had a place for you to stay, which would you do?" Mot flinches a little at the word "homeless," but I imagine him dead beside the damned car if he stays here and I press on. "Is a car like his worth living outside in the July desert?"

The kid takes a closer look at Mot. I can see the moment when he first notices the way the paralysis gives an odd tilt to Mot's shoulders, the broken Dollar Store sunglasses, the stained jacket. "Well, maybe not worth that," he concedes.

Mot's still not convinced. "Hey, you don't know anything about cars. Let me talk to this kid. Leave us alone."

"Okay," I say, but I turn to the kid before I wander off. "You know, if we leave it here, you could probably have the car. I need to stick to my schedule, and we're not going to have time to sell it to a junkyard." I can tell by the look in his eye that I've won, and I'm glad he's too smart to smile and ruin the whole thing.

I meander over to an aisle filled with brightly colored, useless junk like Dale Earnhardt mud flaps and Barbie seat covers and let the boy talk Mot out of buying the things he has piled on the counter. In fifteen minutes we're in my car, headed back to Dale to get what we can out of the trunk of the old sedan. Mot has promised the kid he'll leave the keys and the title under the passenger side seat.

"I probably got ripped off," Mot says as we drive away. "But you said the right word back there. I don't want to get isolated out here." It's the last clue he'll give me about how to make this difficult trip possible for him—one I'll need to pay attention to often over the next few days.

We no longer have a plan, nor do we have a temporary language of signals we can use to bridge the distance between us. For an hour, Mot can't even speak to me. He knocks his forehead rhythmically against the window and stares out at the barren landscape. Even when we drive past the exit for Prague, with its billboards promising blessings for all who come to pray to the Infant Jesus, he's silent as a stone. No question I ask, no story I tell, will get him to open up his mouth and speak. His silence starts to scare me. I've seen Mot in many moods, but not a one of them was quiet. Talk is what keeps him going, he says. Silence can only mean he's listening to the Big Guys Upstairs, and I don't want to be cooped up in a car with Moloch and Dubja for a thousand miles. This seems the sort of moment when they might shove him back down the stairs so they can take over for a while.

I pull off at the first big gas station outside Henryetta, an hour east of Shawnee. I top off the tank and then sneak into the bathroom to call Scotti. I'm afraid that if Mot overheard any argument, even the smallest sign that I had to convince Scotti that I wasn't making a mistake by not leaving Mot in Dale, he'd get out of the car and set out on foot. I needn't have worried. Scotti agrees that the only thing to do is bring Mot home. He tells me to take all the time I need to get back, and not to worry about the extra money for hotel rooms and meals. I recognize the kindness in this and am grateful. I don't let myself believe that he's agreeing to this only so I can't complain about Rita.

"I love you. Just get home safely," Scotti says, "and call me when you can."

I grab two cans of Coors Light from the cooler at the back of the gas station. It goes against everything I've been told by social workers and psychotherapists during my time at Friendship Room, but sometimes alcohol brings Mot back to himself. The guy at the counter gives me a knowing look when he rings me up, and another when I slip one can into my purse and put the other in a brown paper sack. It's a look that says he thinks I am a drunk and that he'd better not see me hanging around outside in the parking lot, a look I imagine Mot must see a lot. Tired and worried, I shrug as I push the door open with my elbow and walk out to the car.

Years of drinking and traveling have made Mot careful. He takes the beer happily but insists that I drive around behind the gas station before he'll drink it. The fact that he has told me what to do feels like a victory. Halfway through the first can he's my Mot again, chatty and examining the events of the day so far. By the time he has finished it, he's comfortable he has made the right decision. He waves away the second beer when I pull it out of my purse.

"Save it," he says in a serious voice. "We're going to need that one, and probably a lot more, if I'm going to go with you on this crazy trip." Then he laughs and puts his arm around my shoulder. "You're a strange one, but maybe that will be a good thing in the end."

My original plan had been to make the drive home in one very long day; with Mot along, there's no chance of that. He can't take sitting in the car for hours at a stretch. His back begins to hurt, the numbness in his left side gets worse, and he grows antsy.

"I usually limit myself to two hundred miles a day, tops," he suggests as we leave Henryetta.

"I don't have six days for the drive. I have to be back at Friendship Room by midweek. Do you think you can make it if we shoot for four hundred miles a day?"

"Probably not." He sighs as he settles down into the passenger seat for a nap. "But I guess there isn't anything to do now but try and see what happens. If I don't make it, what would you do with my body?"

Instead of answering, I tune the radio to a country station and set the cruise control to five miles an hour over the speed limit.

Mot laughs a little. "Yeah, better not to take the bait on that one, kid. Guess you've learned a thing or two after all." He sleeps for the two and a half hours it takes to get from Shawnee to Fort Smith, Arkansas. We're only a little more than two hundred miles from where we began the day, but I'm too weary to keep driving, so we stop at the first likely place on the eastern side of Fort Smith. Maybe, in the end, we will go at Mot's pace. Mine suddenly seems impossible.

We spend the night at a Holiday Inn. I'm less comfortable than I'd been at the campground. Maybe it's the idea of staying in a hotel with a man who isn't my husband, or maybe it's that the bathroom is right there and he lies on one of the beds shouting through the wall while I shower and change. I feel claustrophobic and a little resentful, even though I'm glad Mot's with me instead of stranded in Dale. It's only while I'm hurrying through this shower that I realize how long I'd stood under the endless stream of hot water at the KOAs, making room for silence. Until we are back in Morgantown, or until Mot decides he can't keep going and leaves me at some point along the way, I will have no time for solitude.

And it worries me that we don't have a plan. Mot insists he won't come all the way back to Morgantown with me, but he hasn't decided how far he'll go or where he'd like to stay next. He once lived in Memphis, working the third shift at a warehouse.

"We never got any work done, but the guys were okay. Anytime we wanted, we'd just drop a box of cough syrup. This is back when they used to put good stuff in cough syrup. We'd drink up a few bottles each and leave the mess for the daytime crew. But there was a guy there who wanted to kill me, so I had to leave. I wouldn't want to go back there."

And Kentucky is out, although he doesn't have a reason for that except that it's Kentucky.

"Maybe I'll go as far as Huntington with you," he says. "It would be weird, though, being in a town with your mother and sister. So maybe Charleston. We'll just have to play it by ear."

The next morning, he insists on getting under the hood of my car. "You're running hot," he says. "I still say you need a summer thermostat, but something else is wrong, too."

"The car's not running hot," I insist. "I've been watching the temperature gauge and it hasn't gone above the halfway mark the entire trip." I'm worried that he'll try to fix something that isn't broken, and we'll end up stranded in Arkansas.

"I don't care what the gauge says, something's wrong." He leans in to take a look. "Move the car back out of the parking space." I do, and he points to a fresh puddle of oil on the asphalt. He reaches down and pulls the cap off the oil pump without twisting.

"You got your oil changed right before you made the trip down here?"

he asks. I had. "See, I told you something was wrong. They didn't put the cap back on all the way." He pulls out the dipstick and oil barely coats the tip. "It's a wonder you haven't burned up the engine already!" I don't know if it's coincidence or if he's more tuned to the sounds and smells of engines than I am. The oil pressure light had never come on, the thermostat had never shown that the car was running hot, but his intuition had been right.

The girl at the front desk gives us directions to an AutoZone a few stoplights away, but Mot, needing the reliable familiarity of Walmart, drives us around the outskirts of Fort Smith until we find one. Having been right silences the voices in his head for a while. It's obvious that he's more whole, more in control. He even insists on charging me an Egg McMuffin and a cup of McDonald's coffee for his services. "You gotta feed a man if you're going to expect him to work," he says.

So we stop at McDonald's and then at Walmart. Mot eats his breakfast and pours in the oil, and the morning is already half gone. It's beginning to feel like I'll never get home, like we'll be stuck on the road forever.

As we pass the town of Ozark an hour later, a terrible tiredness grips me. I ask Mot to drive, but he says he needs his first beer of the day. We stop for a while in the parking lot of an abandoned day-care center off the highway. Mot can't take the cold and is glad to get out of the air-conditioned car, but I can't take the heat. Under the oppressive sun, exhaustion bakes into my bones. Mot won't be moved until he's ready, so while he sits on the edge of an empty concrete planter, slowly nursing his beer, I crawl into the backseat to nap. It's like a snapshot of what things would be like if I let his life overtake mine. As I fall asleep, I think again of the line from one of his emails, *There is something here that doesn't want us to get completely totaled without a warning.*

The rest of the day, we travel only in short spurts, stopping every hour and a half so Mot can drink a warm beer and I can catch a quick nap. We don't talk about what to do next or where we are going. At sunset on the second day of the drive, we stop outside Lexington, Kentucky, and eat a dinner of giant, perfect cheeseburgers and fries in a honky-tonk across from a Day's Inn. The music is so loud the waitress can't hear Mot's stupid coffee story, so he gives up halfway through. Although we had planned to get back on the highway, I fall asleep in the booth in spite of the music and the clank of beer bottles everywhere, so we check into the motel instead.

In the morning, I've run out of things to say. Two days of nothing to do but converse have left me without a single untold story or crackpot theory left to fill the silence. Mot, too, has grown quiet, although whether he is out of material or fretting over what to do is impossible to know. It's Sunday. He turns the radio to NPR so we can let Garrison Keillor and Michael Feldman do the talking for us.

Mot says that he often goes months without anyone to talk to and that during those times the people on NPR are as close as he comes to having friends. He likes *Whad'Ya Know* best, but *Car Talk* is the show that's on the local station right now. We listen as a woman named Anne tells Tom and Ray about driving her husband several hundred miles to their home after his surgery to reverse a vasectomy. She wonders if, in her hurry to get him home and comfortable, her relentless pace caused the new, unpleasant noise in her Dodge Caravan. Tom and Ray think not.

"Hey, you should call these guys," Mot insists as the show is winding down. "They'll know about summer and winter thermostats."

"Maybe I should." I reach for my cell phone.

"Sheesh, not while you're driving!" Mot reaches to take the phone from me. "Sometimes I don't know how you've survived this long without me, kiddo."

Within a few hours, we're over the border into West Virginia. I pull off Interstate 64 and drive Mot around Huntington, pointing out the library, the homeless shelter, and the park. I don't show him my mother's house. We go down to the park along the banks of the Ohio and up into the hills outside of town where I think he might be able to camp unmolested if he wants to stay. His small Social Security check isn't enough to cover the cost of an apartment, even in West Virginia. But if he stayed, my mother could help him find subsidized housing and other benefits. This is exactly the sort of social work she does. For a moment, I think this is the best possible solution. "We could stop for the day and you could look around," I offer.

"Let's go on and see Charleston," he says. "I'm not going to Morgantown, I mean, that's for sure. But maybe Charleston would be better than this."

I consider trying to talk him into giving it a try here, but it's possible my mother won't see his charm and he'll be just another difficult case for her already overburdened office. I let it go.

Back on the highway, we drive through towns too small to have homeless shelters or soup kitchens. Mot thinks he could live off what he could forage in the woods and is momentarily taken with the idea of stopping along a part of the highway near no town at all and wandering off into the wilderness. I tell him there is no real wilderness here, pointing out the tire marks of ATVs and the empty beer cans on the hillside. We cross the bridge into Nitro, a town right outside Charleston that was built around chemical refineries and that always smells of bleach and rotten eggs. Mot catches a whiff and decides we should go on to Clarksburg. "A man could die if the wind shifted and he got caught in those fumes!" he insists. And so it is with each town we pass: maybe the next one will be better. Finally, we arrive in Morgantown after all.

We stop at an old room-by-the-week motel at the edge of town where the Friendship Room folk often stay when they're flush. I've put the knowledge that he molested his sister so very long ago as far out of my mind as I can, but that's not so far that I would now move him into my house with my teenage stepdaughter. I give the guy at the desk two hundred dollars. It's toward the end of the month, and Mot's Social Security check is nearly gone. He'll have enough to feed himself but not enough to pay for a place to stay, and I can't handle the idea of throwing him back into the community of the homeless shelter and Friendship Room. I'm escaping. So should he.

"This will buy us a week to figure out what to do next," I tell Mot. Together, we move the few things he scavenged from the sedan into a small room that smells of stale cigarette smoke and mold. When I turn to go, he grabs my hand.

"Thanks for not leaving me back there in Oklahoma," he says quietly. "I don't think I'll be here long, but it's better than being stuck at the only gas station in Dale." I kiss him on the cheek and get into my car.

Scotti and I don't fight about my paying for Mot to move into the motel, although money is tight and about to get more so. I have only two weeks left at Friendship Room and no other job in sight. We do fight about money if I want to buy a new pair of shoes, go out to dinner, or come home from the bookstore with more than one book. He doesn't complain about my relationship with Mot because it mirrors his relationship with Rita. He spends hours every day with her and more hours on the phone in the evening, and sometimes he skips our family holidays so that he can go with her to her mother's house in a small coal-mining town an hour and a half away. Scotti told me when we first married that he hid his finances from his last wife in part because she complained about the money he spent on Rita, so I know he buys her things, and I think he sometimes pays her bills. This last, I have no way of knowing. We keep our finances separate, though he notices where my money goes. I make so little it's barely enough for groceries and gas. He pays for everything else. But I don't know how much he makes, except that his salary is not enough to keep up with the debts he acquired during his mother's long battle with Alzheimer's and his embattled divorce from Lucy's mother.

Our fights about Rita have grown more bitter. Before I married Scotti, she and I were friends, but she shielded me from the worst of her symptoms, as she does with most people. Since I married Scotti, she has gradually come to see me as an extension of him and so has begun to subject me to the anger and vitriol that are part of her illness. She threatens to burn or cut or kill herself if she calls and I can't immediately put him on the phone. She announces that she is running away, sometimes after she is already in the car and uncertain where she is at the moment, running blind from something that isn't really there. And of course, there was the phone call in which I could hear her nephews crying in the background as she threatened to kill them.

I want this to stop. I want Scotti to stay home for our Thanksgiving and Christmas dinners instead of spending them with Rita and her broken family. I want to be able to travel without him spending hours on the phone with her while I sit in the hotel room, waiting for her to calm down so that we can go out. I don't want to have to tell Lucy repeatedly that of course she is more important to him but that Rita needs him more right now, because I don't think the latter is true. Lucy is thirteen and having a hard time coping with her parents' divorce, though she never takes this out on me. She yells at Scotti over tiny things, but she has been welcoming and kind to me from the beginning. She clearly needs him as much as Rita does, and I am angry that he doesn't see that. And I too want to matter more than Rita does, though it has become apparent that I never will.

Mot's presence makes it harder for me to hold my ground in this fight. Now each of us has a friend whose pathologies take precedence over a quiet evening at home together or a weekend away. Maybe this is why he doesn't mind. Or maybe he's genuinely more generous of spirit than I am. Either way, Mot's moving to Morgantown will cost me this particular battle. I know it, so I stop fighting. I stop complaining about being lonely and about coming after Rita on Scotti's list of priorities. Home becomes an easier place to be, and that's a welcome change. But it also widens the gulf between us, which was already so great that I often can't remember what I loved about him when we first married.

HOME

And if your brother be waxen poor, and fallen in decay
with you; then you shall relieve him: yes, though he be
a stranger, or a sojourner; that he may live with you.
—Leviticus 25:35

Mot has agreed to stay awhile and is moving into an apartment. It's a dump, with walls of cheap plywood paneling over bare studs and the musty smell of a carpet laid directly on a damp concrete floor. But it's on the bus line, there's a laundry room where the washers cost only fifty cents and the dryers a quarter, and the rent's less than four hundred dollars a month with all utilities included. It's also better than the motel room, which is damp and cold even in the heat of August. His neighbors on the left at the motel are a family of five who send their toddlers out to play in the parking lot all day while the parents drink; his neighbor on the right is an aging prostitute who has taken a shine to him. In the apartment on Breezy Drive, his immediate neighbors will be a man the landlord says can but doesn't speak and one of the local high school's soccer coaches. "A better class of crazies," Mot calls them.

The night before he moves into the apartment, like almost every night since we got back to town, we go to Walmart. Mot still needs the comfort of this familiar ritual and calls often to say there's something he must have that can be gotten only at Walmart: a particular brand of razor, a two-pack of WD-40, balsam shampoo, sardines in mustard. So we go, walking the aisles long after we've found what we have come to find, until he feels okay.

This time, we're buying lightbulbs. "I noticed the ones in the apartment are only forty-watters, and I like seventy-five. Light's important, you know." It's the only preparation he has made to move into the new place. He hasn't shown much enthusiasm for the idea of living indoors. He has made it clear that he's really taking the apartment for my sake so I won't worry so much. And he's right that his being indoors eases my worries. Winter is coming, and sixty-six seems too old to be planning to weather the out-of-doors. I want walls for him, a furnace, and a warm bed.

I watch him go up and down the aisles. Holding on to the shopping cart, he doesn't limp, and only a very careful observer would notice his right side dragging his left along. He is clean, his clothes are freshly laundered, and he looks more like a retired professor than a homeless man. No one gives him a second glance until he begins to push his cart aggressively between two chatting women who are blocking the lightbulb aisle. Then he looks crazy, even dangerous. The women pull back and shake their heads. He barrels ahead and then waits for me to catch up, sneaking sidelong glances at me to see if I'm angry or embarrassed. I'm not, although this acceptance is something I've had to learn.

We stand staring at generic lightbulbs. Mot trembles and is quiet for a few minutes and then reaches out and takes a box of two seventy-five-watt bulbs from the display. "I am now someone who needs lightbulbs," he says in a very quiet voice. At first I think this is some peculiar trick of his illness, that there must be a secret meaning to lightbulbs that I haven't yet uncovered in our conversations. "This is the first time in forty years I've needed to buy lightbulbs," he says, surreptitiously wiping his eyes on his shirt cuff.

Finally I get it. He's struggling with the idea of home, mourning the ones he hasn't had and coming to terms with the idea of settling for this one, at least for now. I pretend to be studying a nearby display until he puts the bulbs in the cart and shambles toward the checkout lines. There are days when the crazy tries to beat me up, when everything he says is such twisty nonsense it gives me a headache. Days when I want to shake him, to say, "If you know you're nuts, why do you still believe this delusional bullshit?" Days when I wonder why we are friends. This is not one of those days. This is a day when complex problems might have simple solutions, when buying lightbulbs at Walmart is a real victory over the darkness.

It's clear the landlord didn't clean the apartment after the last tenant left. There are some things we're glad to have: a bed, a heavy Naugahyde sofa so old it's campy, and a set of metal shelves. Other things I think should be thrown away but Mot insists on keeping: frozen hamburger patties and turkey hotdogs encased in a layer of frost in the freezer, a set of dubious-looking sheets, and a stack of disposable plastic plates that have clearly been used, rinsed, and put back in the cupboards. There are a few things we can agree need to be tossed: a half box of condoms left on the back of the toilet, a moldy shower curtain, a used bar of soap, several disintegrating lumps in the refrigerator. I'm relieved to see that there's a line even Mot won't cross. I was afraid he'd decide the used bar of soap was worth saving.

We spend the first day cleaning. Mot's car was always full of half-eaten cans of things, empty beer bottles, old newspapers, unexplained coils of aquarium tubing, and dirty laundry. By his own report, when he's camping or living out of a car it's often many days—even, I think, sometimes weeks—between opportunities to shower. But with a place to call home, he becomes fastidious. He moves the appliances so we can scrub the floor under them, something it has never occurred to me to do in my own home. Light fixtures come down to be washed, screens are pulled from the windows, and cabinet doors are unhinged. He takes a broken vacuum cleaner from the dumpster, fixes it, and insists I go over the rugs at least three times. Everything gets soaked in or scrubbed with bleach. My hands are red and raw by the time we're done.

A dangerous amount of hope swirls around us, but we aren't forgetful of history. Before Mot signs the lease, we both tell the landlord that his health might not allow him to stay for the entire year. I have no idea if the landlord can tell that by health, we mean that Mot is nuts. He seems unconcerned, though. This looks like the sort of place where lots of tenants skip out without paying their back rent, and he says it won't be a problem as long as he gets thirty days' notice. Mot says, "Well, sure," and signs the paperwork, even though we both know that if he decides to go, he won't wait thirty days to do it.

Mot also talks himself into a job. He walks the landlord around the building, pointing out things that need a good scrubbing and wood that should be repainted before winter, showing off the vacuum cleaner he repaired. The landlord, looking at the unhinged cabinet doors and freshly scrubbed floors, offers Mot minimum wage to do the things he has suggested and to keep the lawn cut. He won't pay him, per se, but he'll take the amount Mot earns off his rent each month. Since we're splitting the cost of the apartment, Mot could end up paying nothing if he can stretch the work out to twenty-eight hours a month. A free place to live would make his modest income enough to live a reasonably comfortable life.

This is a day where everything Mot needs is within his grasp: a job, a place to live, a community that welcomes him, companionship. It can't be this simple, so I start looking for signs of trouble beneath the surface. He hasn't mentioned or seemed distracted by the Others all day. Surely they wouldn't miss such a big event? There are so many opportunities here for paranoia and discontent. The Others worry me most when they are conspicuously absent. I can't help Mot pick truth from delusion when I don't know what they're whispering to him.

I'm spending most of my time putting Mot's life in order, and it's starting to become too much even for Scotti. He grumbles about dinners that don't get cooked, floors that don't get mopped, clothes that don't get washed. He can't insist that I cut down on my time with Mot, though, because his days are just as busy taking care of Rita. We are making one another unhappy because we are each more involved with someone else than with each other, and neither of us is willing to change that. We are stalemated.

Mot begins to fall apart if I don't spend at least a few hours with him each day. He doesn't need me to clean or cook. In fact, he prefers that I don't help with the chores around the apartment because I don't do them to his exacting standards. I put too much salt in the food; I'm not careful enough about getting into the corners when I sweep the floors. What he needs is company and help acquiring the necessities to live indoors. Furniture, food, books. Curtains and blankets, pots and pans. Help arranging for an Internet connection so he can use the laptop at night. Rides to Walmart.

It occurs to me that I may have accidentally become the wife of two difficult men, with two households to run, though I was already failing as the wife of only one. I am not cut out for being the person who attends to the minutiae of everyday life—laundry and shopping and making certain the bills are paid. Now, all I have time for is attending to these things, and nothing ever seems to get done quickly enough, or it's done the wrong way, and both men are surprised when I say I am overwhelmed. "But you're not really doing anything right now," they both say.

But of course I'm doing lots of things, just nothing that either thinks worth his notice. My job at Friendship Room has finally come to an end, and instead of finding another one, I'm taking classes to finish my undergraduate degree. I thought I'd graduated in the midnineties, and I would have had I known there was a fee to pay and an application to complete. At the time, I was anxious to get school out of the way so that I could move to Alabama and marry Jimmy, my second husband. In the rush to move on to the next part of my life, I hadn't paid enough attention to the administrative details. When no diploma came, I assumed it was simply because I hadn't given the university my Alabama address and the post office hadn't forwarded the diploma from my previous address. It never occurred to me that I might not have actually graduated, and for years I'd been putting the BA I never earned on résumés and working in jobs that it turns out I wasn't technically qualified to do. I discovered the truth only two years ago when signing up for a writing workshop at the university, and now I'm recuperating from Friendship Room in the easier world of academia.

The requirements for the degree have changed in the decade and a half since I left school, so I need three more hours of a science and nine more hours of electives to graduate. I am taking Geology 101, a social work class, and six hours of creative writing. My days should be spent reading and churning out essays. Instead, my time is split between two very demanding men and my own life, which is already overfull. I volunteer my time to agencies I hope will hire me once the semester is over, trying not to fall so far off out of that sphere that it's hard to find a job when I'm ready to go back to work. My afternoons are often spent taking Lucy to and from all the places a teenage girl has to go: the mall, soccer practice, a friend's house, the mall again. Shuttling Lucy becomes the part of my day I most look forward to: our talks in the car, our silliness, our outings together. My life with Scotti is filled with half-finished projects, unharvested gardens, and unmet expectations. Mot's life is empty except for what I bring to it. Left on his own, he sits alone in his apartment listening to the *Big Guys Upstairs* and growing miserable in a new way.

Within a few days of his moving into the apartment, it's clear that Mot is not meant to live this way. Without the challenges of living out of doors, he's bored, and his illness uses the empty hours to create increasingly elaborate delusions. He has begun talking about the Rosicrucians and Knights Templar, printing out maps of modern-day Israel and covering them with cryptic symbols he refuses to explain. He's growing cagier about the attacks by the *Big Guys Upstairs*, and not knowing the details makes me less useful as a bridge to the real. Too much of what he has hoped for is now present in his life, and he says this makes what isn't present—family, friends, a real place in the community—harder to live without. But I want to believe that our friendship is strong enough to make it possible for him to stay through the winter, at least, and so I look for reasons to be hopeful instead of signs that he has the urge for going before he has even settled in.

Lucy is the only person in either household that I love easily and without reservation. We sit in the kitchen and gossip about junior high school while I make dinner; we watch Disney shows in the evening that I'm surprised she hasn't outgrown. She is particularly fond of the shows about happy, intact families, and together we try to become one. Somehow our relationship survives her anger over her parents' divorce. Scotti and I have failed to gel as a couple, but Lucy and I adore one another fiercely.

When Mot left my house the first time, everything he owned fit into the child's book bag that was all he could manage to carry. We were able to salvage enough of what he'd acquired to fill the trunk of my car when we left the sedan in Oklahoma, most of it more talismanic than pragmatic. He has almost none of the things that make living in an apartment possible. Mot needs pots, pans, spices, sheets, pillows, chairs, a radio, and houseplants. The plants are his first priority. "Imagine if we could superoxygenate this environment!" he insists excitedly. "I could probably grow ten years younger!" I have no idea if he means that literally or metaphorically.

We buy ferns and daisies at Walmart and a giant ficus at Lowe's. Our daily shopping journeys now include hardware stores, where we borrow tools at least as often as we buy them. When Mot decides he needs Sheetrock to build a computer desk, he takes a T square and a knife from other aisles, props the Sheetrock on a dolly, and begins to measure and cut right there in the store. I almost say something about how a desk made of Sheetrock will never hold up, but then I remember that Mot does not like to create permanent things. It feels too risky to him. He's afraid of leaving a part of himself behind, though he can't or won't say why. And while I'm not sure if dulling the blade on a knife we don't intend to buy is even the pettiest of larcenies, this scene makes me uncomfortable. Even Mot seems to realize we've crossed the line. He alternates between ordering me to hold my end of the Sheetrock steady and giving me instructions on how to get away with this. "Don't look anyone in the eye," he says, "and should anyone ask if we need help, just smile and say, 'Thanks, but we got it.' Trust me, they won't bother us." He watches me as closely as he watches the work. This is a test.

It takes us twenty minutes to turn the unmanageable piece of Sheetrock into a manageable stack of carefully measured pieces cut into the shapes of a desk top, shelves, and a pedestal. Mot has told me stories about working on construction sites, but never with the detail I'd expect from a skilled tradesperson. Most of the stories were about drinking with the other guys at work, getting fired, or taking off because the boss said one thing or another that rubbed him the wrong way. But a more competent and whole Mot emerges as he measures and cuts. He's clearly a man who has done these things before and knows what he's doing. This isn't the imagined Mot of the steakhouse or the long drives. He suddenly has skill, speed, and an economy of movement that comes only with great practice. This was once the person who lived in his body—one of the ones, I'm almost certain, who called himself "Tom" and lived without any awareness of the *Big Guys Upstairs*.

According to Mot, he discovered the *Others* when he trekked the Mojave Desert, trying to make himself whole by mimicking Christ's fast of forty days and forty nights. If I ask when that was, he'll say three years ago. But again there is a trick. If I ask how old he was when he went into the Mojave, he won't tell me, but he'll suddenly change his story a little. "It was about fifteen years ago, I think," he'll say to dodge the question about his age, and this timing fits better with the other stories he's told me about his life. He enrolled in the University of Vermont about ten years ago, and between semesters he began to travel the world. His stories from before then mostly take place in the United States, and they are most often about the unusual jobs he had. He worked once in a laboratory where chemicals of some sort were tested on chicks. It was his job to clean the cages and euthanize the birds once they were no longer needed. A very long time ago, he worked for NCR and sold early computer equipment in Greenland. He did a stint in the army, though he makes no claim to have been in combat. He says he served during the Korean War, though the math doesn't work for that. He would have been only thirteen when the armistice was signed. I don't believe he's lying, though; I think he's just mistaken. I know he served because I've seen his VA card, and I know he is the age he claims because I've seen his driver's license. Mostly, it seems, in his previous life he built things.

Watching him cut the drywall, I can imagine Mot becoming again a less troubled, more functional version of himself. Clearly, he has skills the landlord would be thrilled to have for minimum wage, and he could easily earn his share of the rent every month. And he seems engaged in the tasks around him. He spent yesterday scrubbing his neighbors' stoops with bleach and building a corner plant stand from some plywood he found in a scrap heap. I try to make myself believe that Breezy Drive is the perfect place for him after all.

On good days, when I have time and Mot feels well enough, we add junk shops and the Salvation Army to our acquisitive journeys. He won't go to Goodwill, although he says he can't remember why. We buy very little. We spend most of our time picking up the oddest of the objects and trying to re-create the lives of their previous owners. He is much better at the game than I am, willing to give the imagined people more tragic lives and to imbue the objects with greater meaning.

"This rather distressed print of the famous painting *Blue Boy* hung for years over the mantle of the recently deceased Miss Doris Jarvis. Miss Jarvis, known as 'Dori the Whore-y' to the other regulars at the Dew Drop Inn, never in her eighty-seven years gave up on finding true love and having a family of her own. In the last decade of her life, it seems she actually came to believe this was a picture of her son and, when she had a little too much to drink, took to berating it for birthday cards it never sent her and what a rat bastard of a son it had been, really, now that she thought about it," Mot said, holding up the dingy, cobwebbed print as if it were something rotten. "Miss Jarvis's only heir, a great-grandniece named Miss Kimberly Dawn Fredeking, felt the painting would clash with her collection of Metallica posters and NASCAR memorabilia, so donated it to the Salvation Army along with a large collection of Avon perfume bottles shaped like Disney princesses and several pairs of gold lamé sandals."

I suggest that a bitter divorce may be behind the set of golf clubs that looks too new for the Salvation Army and attribute a busted television screen to an overzealous football fan, but I can't weave stories that compare with the epic tragedies Mot pulls from insignificant pieces of junk. And then I think that he might be better off if he, too, could come up with only trite, likely tales.

The few things we do buy are real finds. One is a pair of lattice-backed chairs with delicately carved feet and awful pink flowered material poorly upholstered to their cushioned seats. Mot upends the chairs and shows me the supports that were added long after the chairs were made, the minor damage done when the original seats were removed. "These are good chairs, though," he says, running his fingers over the joint in the wood where leg meets seat, "and probably a hundred years old. See, you have to learn to look for the lines of things. Most folks would look at these and just see that ugly material, but color and pattern will fool you. You have to find the bones of something to know if it's any good." I buy them along with two remnants of damask upholstery fabric we find in a bin full of old sheets. Neither one of us knows how to fix the chairs, but I'm certain Mot will have figured it out before I pick him up tomorrow morning.

TASHLIKH

He will take us back in love;
He will cover up our iniquities,
You will hurl all our sins
Into the depths of the sea.
—Micah 7:19

The grapevines are overburdened with fruit, ripe and fragrant. I don't know what to do with the bounty. Before the vines are divested of even half their burden, I have put up dozens of jars of jelly, more than Scotti and I can use or give away. Mot suggests that we make wine.

Mot insists that we cut the grapes from the vines with pruning shears instead of simply breaking off the bunches by twisting the stems, as I have always done, and he pulls the intertwined snakeweed from the arbor. He can't recall ever having done migrant farmwork but acknowledges that he knows a surprising amount about how to harvest grapes for someone with no experience at it. By lunchtime, we have ten paper grocery bags full of ripe fruit and purple stains on our hands and faces. "Enough!" Mot announces. "We've picked too many."

"We haven't taken a third of what's here," I say, gesturing to the fruit still left. "What am I going to do with all of this?"

"That, lady, eez not my problem," Mot says with a flourish. "My job is just to make zee wine." He picks up a bag and begins to walk toward the car. "Come along, come along! We have grapes to stomp!"

We don't, of course, stomp them. Back at his apartment, we experiment with different ways of smashing them. First, we put them by bunches into a large mixing bowl and then, using a glass soda bottle as a pestle, try to grind the juice out of them. But the walls of the bowl are slick, and the slip-skin fruit shoots out across the kitchen when pressed. Next, we fill up a large pasta pot and, out of doors this time, drop a cheesecloth-wrapped brick on top of the grapes until we have a pulpy mess.

"Wait," Mot says as the mess splashes out onto the walkway. "I remember how we did this." He pauses, looking sheepish.

"Okay, then, tell me. This clearly isn't working."

"We bought frozen grape juice concentrate." He ducks his head, then looks at me sideways. "I mean, I remembered we started with grape juice, so I just assumed we got it from grapes."

I look up at him, grape pulp in my hair, on my shirt, under my fingernails, and laugh. "What? You are kidding me, right?" I shake the goo from my fingers back into the pasta pot. "What are we going to do with fifty pounds of grapes?" And then the answer is immediately obvious.

"Grape fight!" I grab handfuls of fruit from the paper sacks. Mot peppers me with individual grapes. I toss an entire bunch. I grab the pot and begin chasing him around the building.

"Hey, now!" he says, sliding down the hill toward the laundry room. "No fair using the smashed ones! You'll ruin my shirt, probably dye my hair purple!"

I hold the pot above his head. The run downhill had been a strategic error on his part, ceding the high ground to me. "Say uncle!" I taunt him by sloshing the grape slurry until it almost spills over the sides.

"What?" he asks, suddenly serious.

"Surrender!" I tilt the pot a little, still caught up in the game.

"I think you should go home now." Mot stands up, dusts himself off, and walks into the apartment, locking the door behind him.

I stand stunned for a moment and then clean up the mess, hoping Mot will open the door when he hears me puttering around on the stoop. But he doesn't, and so I don't knock. Once the grapes and the pots are in a neat pile by his door, I get in my car and drive home. I know what I've done, can't believe I was dumb enough to do it, and don't know how to fix it.

Mot's abusers have all been women: his murderous mother, his aunts, and Brunhilda, the petty and vicious housekeeper who was brought in to care for Mot and his siblings while his mother was hospitalized. *I hated everything about her but her smell. She smelled lovely, in a way that I didn't understand when I was a boy,* he says when he talks about her. But he also says, *She picked us off, one by one, and she was more frightening than our mother because she was more cunning and just as vicious.* I know all of this, but sometimes I don't make the connections quickly enough to avoid stepping into the expected role. There is nothing to do now but wait to see if this is the thing that will break us or if we can get past it.

In the morning, I head for Mot's at the usual time, hoping that if I act as if nothing has happened, it will be as if nothing has. But I'm not halfway there when my cell phone rings.

"Where are you?" Mot asks.

"I'm on my way. I should be there in about ten minutes."

"No, don't come. I was hoping I'd catch you before you left home. I don't think I should see you anymore. I mean, this isn't good for me."

"I don't understand." I know what he means, but unable to think of the right thing to say, I try to buy a little time.

"Look, I'm sorry, but I have to do what's best for me. And that is to get out of here. What you want from me, I don't have to give. I don't want to blame you. That wouldn't be nice. But you're not a good person for me to be around."

I don't have an answer to this. I don't even know that he's wrong. The only thing I can think of is that he has my geology book, and there is a test tomorrow.

"Okay, but can you let me come by and pick up my textbooks? I won't bother you, and if you don't want to talk to me you don't have to, but I have an exam."

Mot's too kind to say *no.* "All right, then, come on. I mean, I don't want you to, but I'm not going to stand in the way of your education. I don't want to be that guy."

By the time I get to the apartment, I've convinced myself that it's best to let him go without an argument. Not because I want to but because of how badly I don't. We are friends. And if we are to remain so, I must treat him with respect and honor his choices. Because I can't say that his staying is better for him, not just better for me, I'm determined not to stand in his way.

As soon as I'm in the door, though, he no longer thinks he needs to go. "Look," he says, standing in a corner with his arms wrapped around himself protectively. "Maybe we can still be pals or something. I just wish you were a guy. Then this would be normal." He gives me a look full of apprehension. "Do you know what I mean?"

"I know what you mean. Pals is good. Pals is best, in fact." I reach out and then realize that hugging is probably not the way to cement this agreement, so I pull back one arm. "Shake on it?"

He sets his mouth in a grim line. "No," he says. "I mean, I wish you were a guy, but you're not. So no handshakes." I don't know what this means—if handshakes are for men only, or if even a handshake with a woman is too risky for him right now. But it doesn't matter. I nod and put my hand in my pocket.

"I need to go to Walmart," he says after a moment of awkward silence. "The toilet leaks and I need to get a new seal for it." So we go to Walmart, not quite but almost as if nothing has happened.

Early on in our friendship, Mot said, "I should have put an ad in the *New Yorker* a long time ago. 'Goy seeks Jew. Must have a sense of humor and a helmet.' I knew it would take a Jewess to get through this mess. Christians all want to be saved once they know there is a Jesus over here. But you can stand up, make a confrontation. And I bet you're hell in a fight."

This is a complicated compliment. Although baptized in the Mennonite church three years ago, I was raised Jewish, and despite how enthusiastically I've embraced the theology of my new faith, I haven't fully let go of the ritual and tradition of my heritage. So I don't say, "I'm not a Jew, not anymore, not really." He knows, of course, but dismisses my conversion as irrelevant.

"You can't stop being a Jew any more than you could stop being a Cherokee. If you were one, I mean. If you were a Cherokee and you converted from whatever-the-heck thing Cherokees believe in to, say, Presbyterianism, would you suddenly be a WASP? No. So, you're a Jew." He means this, too, as a compliment, despite the anti-Semitism of the *Big Guys Upstairs*. In fact, their hatred for my kind is proof against my being in league with them and offers me some protection against his paranoia.

Now, things are strained between us. We haven't fully recovered from the debacle of the grape fight, and Mot is wary when we're together. Today is Rosh Hashanah, the day for asking forgiveness. I've come this morning with a plan.

"Do you know about Tashlikh?" I ask Mot when I pick him up.

"Never heard of it. What is it, some kind of ceremonial food?"

It's a good guess; Jewish holidays are usually about stories and food. "No. It's a Jewish ritual. We throw bread crumbs from our pockets onto moving water, a symbolic way to cast off the mistakes of the past year and start the new afresh. At Rosh Hashanah, we ask forgiveness of one another for the sins of the past year and then cast off our transgressions by throwing bread crumbs into a stream or river." This is an oversimplified explanation, but I don't want to give Mot enough theology to allow the *Big Guys Upstairs* to weave a new delusion from it.

"That sounds nuts," he says.

I hand him a baggie of bread crumbs from my kitchen; another is tucked into the pocket of my jeans. "Well, it can't hurt, can it? I mean, how about this: I come asking you to forgive me for all the ways I have wronged you without intending to in this year. Will you at least forgive me?"

Mot glares at me for a long moment and then shakes his head. "I don't think I'm a man who carries around grudges. I mean, where did that ever get anybody? But I'm not going to go around just forgiving people, either. If you've done bad things to me, well then, you'll just have to live with that."

I don't know what to say. I want to argue the point, but I can see I've come up against something that really has nothing to do with me.

"Look," Mot says, "why should a person forgive the people who hurt him? If I were going to forgive anyone, it should be my own people, my family, but I can't forgive them. Look what they did to me. And if I can't forgive them, why should I forgive you?" He studies me, as if weighing my intentions anew. This is going nowhere.

"Okay, then, bad idea. I have those. But in any case, I forgive you for any small wrongs you've done to me over the past year."

Mot shoots me an angry look and then shakes his head, clearly losing patience with me. "Look, I don't want your damned forgiveness. I haven't done anything to you. What are you trying to say? That you think I've done something that needs to be forgiven? Well, I haven't. And if I had, I'd own up to it and make it right, not ask you to forgive me. I'd fix it. Just drop it, okay?"

I'm stunned by how very wrong I was to imagine that this might be a way to heal the damage done by asking him to surrender during the grape fight. I say simply, "Okay." The misunderstandings usually get worse when I try to clarify, so now I choose silence.

Mot frowns at me for several minutes and then breaks the silence with, "Look, I want to buy a printer. I can't keep using the one at the library. It's too expensive, and besides, I'm tired of that nosy librarian. She always looks at the pages before she hands them to me. I've been having a lot of dreams lately about the death mask of Agamemnon. Do you know who the Knights Templar are?"

"I think so. They fought in the Crusades, right?"

"Oh, they're a lot more than that. But anyway, I think that maybe I'm supposed to find the death mask, that they've got it in a secret location and that's how they're keeping me from getting control back by making me lug these thugs around with me. I saw the mask once; it was a glint on a hillside in Israel. I thought I should get off the bus when we passed by it, but we were in the West Bank and it didn't seem safe. I think I have to go back to find it. There are some articles about the Knights Templar and some more maps of Israel on the Internet that I want to print out. Let's go to Walmart. I saw an ad for a printer that's only twenty-five bucks and I want to buy one. You can use it for your schoolwork, too. You'll be able to print stuff out here."

The mixture of illness and pragmatism makes my head spin. I don't know what's happening. It has been weeks since his delusions were so vivid, so directive. I play along, although I suspect it's the wrong thing to do. But I've lost my leverage, having squandered it on a silly plan to try to trick his illness into forgetting the tension of the last week. And I am heartened, at least, that he says he'll share the printer with me. Perhaps our friendship isn't yet broken beyond repair.

Once Mot is home and the printer is set up, I drive by myself to the park along the Monongahela River. There are small groups of homeless men at the edges of the park, gathered around the benches and public restrooms. Many I recognize from Friendship Room, and a few frighten me. The man who threatened me in Kroger is sitting on a bench with the wife he'd beaten in front of the building, holding her hand. The old marine who pushed me down the fire escape is arguing with two men I don't recognize, grasping a bottle in a brown paper bag and gesticulating wildly. Silently, I forgive each of them and ask just as silently for their forgiveness. I'm not brave enough to speak and don't imagine they'd have much to say. Now that I can neither help nor punish these men, I imagine I'm as insignificant to them as they are to the middle-class women in fleece jackets and leggings walking the nearby trail.

I stand on an old wooden bridge and cast my crumbs into the water. My prayer for forgiveness is a wordless one. I don't have the wisdom to know which parts of myself to cast off and which to keep. I put my faith in God, asking him to choose from among my many flaws. The carp rise up and nibble the bread that floats in an eddy near the bank.

THE SECRET OF THE
AQUARIUM TUBING

Since at the beginning and end of our lives we are so
dependent on others' kindness, how can it be in the middle
that we would neglect kindness towards others?
—**The Dalai Lama**

It's another Walmart day, about a week after the
grape fight, but this time I'm the one creating a scene. People in the adjoining aisles are starting to stare at us. Mot's trying to stand up, and I keep pushing him back down. "Take it *again*," I demand, holding him in the chair in front of the blood pressure cuff. "That can't be right." The screen is blinking 193/116.

"It's right, I told you, it's high. It's been that high for a month now," he says. "I'm going to cut back on my salt some more, and exercise helps."

"Are you fucking kidding me?" I demand, jamming his arm back into the cuff. A woman with two toddlers storms away from us, and I almost hope she comes back with a manager or the pharmacist because we need an objective third person. "Your blood pressure has been this high for a *month* and you haven't done anything about it but lower your salt? Do you have any idea how insane that is?"

"All right, just stop yelling," he whispers. "Jeez, you don't have to get obscene." The word *fucking* bothers him more than the word *insane*. The numbers are slightly higher the second time, no doubt because I'm yelling at him. "If it stays this high I'll go to Health Right next week." Health Right is a free clinic next to Friendship Room that sees the homeless without an appointment on Wednesday afternoons. This is Wednesday evening, and Mot seems to have forgotten that for the moment at least, he's no longer homeless.

"You can't wait a *week* to see someone about this! We're going to the emergency room right now." I do my best to look stern instead of scared. "Please. This is not high blood pressure, this is ten minutes from having a stroke." I go from chiding to beseeching.

Abruptly, he stops arguing. "Okay, have it your way, we'll go," he says, standing up and shuffling toward the exit. It all starts to feel like a setup. Mot and I have walked past the blood pressure cuff almost every day. He has rarely used it, and never when I was around to see the result. The whole event now feels manufactured, as if Mot wanted to go to the ER all along but, for whatever reason, needed to be compelled.

In triage, his blood pressure reads 215/121. These are magic numbers. He is suddenly the focus of great attention and efficiency. Surprisingly, he gives a complete medical history with no delusional embellishment. It's good to hear him sounding so clear, but it's also terrifying. The doctors are treating him like a man they could tell to follow up with his personal physician and trust that it would happen. This sudden burst of rational thinking could, I fear, kill him.

I've been asked who I am, and although I knew *daughter* would be the more effective lie, I opted for cousin. I thought that his vanity would be offended if I acknowledged the twenty-five-year gap in our ages, and that the doctors would then expect me to know things I don't. The truth is an impossibility. If I'd said simply *a friend*, they would have ushered me into the waiting room. I've gone for the manageable lie, but it has given me very little credibility. When I follow the attending physician out of the room and try to explain why it's not safe to simply tell Mot to see his regular doctor, he's dismissive. "Thomas seems fine to me. I'm sure we can get his blood pressure down and send him home with some medications and a referral," he says. "Don't worry about it so much." He brushes me off as a busybody, so I track down his nurse.

Although I know it's disloyal, I explain to her why they have to admit him and keep him under supervision until the crisis has passed. I tell her about the *Big Guys Upstairs*, the *Harpies*, and what little I know about why his file is red-flagged at the Veterans Administration. I think of the waitresses and store clerks I have willed to see past his craziness and am dismayed to find myself in the position of exaggerating his illness to this young woman. He has picked the worst possible time to go sane.

Luckily, my betrayal, though painful, is effective, and they admit him. I expect a fight, but once again there isn't one. He's cooperative, clear-headed. I begin to wonder if he has been playing up his craziness all along to keep me interested. My Mot would never say, "The paralysis might have been a stroke, the last doctor I saw wasn't sure, but it's not the result of the spinal surgery." My Mot thinks it's caused by a device attached to the end of his penis on another plane of existence, something that looks like the front half of a dolphin that the rest of us could see if only we had interdimensional eyes, but whose function he never explains. The man in the bed both is and isn't my friend. Maybe it's Tom. I don't know.

Mot is taken aback when, once he's upstairs, I ask the nurse if she'll have a sleeping chair brought in. "You're going to *stay?*" he asks incredulously. "Why? I mean, it's not like I can bust out of here." He points to the IV hanging from a pole over his head. "And even when I was a kid, no one ever spent the night with me if I had to stay in the hospital. I don't need you hanging around here," he grumbles, but his eyes twinkle and he's smiling.

"I know," I say, "but I'm staying anyway." This is my Mot again, the one who says the opposite of what he means and makes me work to find the truth of things. I'm glad to have him back, although I feel guilty about liking him better when he is less clear. "Besides, they gave you a sedative. I'm hoping you'll shut up and fall asleep so I can finally get some work done." I have brought along my laptop and geology textbook, mostly for show. I don't really want Mot to shut up or believe I'll get any work done. But today has been too raw for outright affection. We have to settle for grousing familiarity.

Mot is a lousy patient. Every time a nurse comes in the room he fades back into his blankets, a passive lump. He has missed dinner but won't tell the nurse; he gripes at me when I ask her to order a tray for him, and he rolls his eyes when I tell her he doesn't eat pork and is on a low-sodium diet. "Jeez, you're bossy!" he complains. But he eats everything as soon as the tray is brought, and then he says he's still hungry and eats the orange

I've been carrying around in my purse all day and had planned to have for my own dinner.

While he eats, I step outside to call Scotti. He isn't angry or even surprised. He sometimes has to spend several hours in the hospital's emergency room with Rita because she can't tolerate being there alone. I am both relieved and a little put out that he doesn't mind. I want us both to stop living the most important parts of our lives with other people.

By eight o'clock, Mot's blood pressure has dropped to 130/84 and everyone relaxes. The doctors have found a combination of medicines that works, and luckily they are all on the four-dollar generic list at Walmart. Once he fills the first scripts, he'll be able to get refills at any of the store's pharmacies.

In the hospital, the mystery of the aquarium tubing is solved. Mot has been using it to catheterize himself. I'm horrified by the difference between the thin, sterile catheters the hospital provides and the relatively thick, rigid homemade ones he carries around in his pockets. I admire his ingenuity, and I hope the loss of feeling that plagues his paralyzed side also protects him from what must otherwise be a terribly painful process. Some things a person should be able to count on, and if you need them, a clean supply of catheters should be one of those things.

While Mot's finishing his dinner, I excuse myself to go to the bathroom and sneak out to the nurses' station. I explain Mot's situation and ask if they could give me a week's supply of catheters while I figure out where and how to buy them. His nurse refuses to give me even a few and instead harangues me for having asked, as if they are expensive things and the cost of them would come directly out of her paycheck. I'm shocked at her vehemence, but in the end I have to agree with her when she insists that I've asked her to steal catheters from the hospital. Chastised, I slink back to my sleeping chair to wait for the next shift.

"So, I hope you're not embarrassed," I say once he's done eating, "but I think we should get you a supply of real catheters. I asked the nurse for some to take home, but she was pretty Nurse Ratched–y about it."

He clearly is embarrassed. "No, don't worry about it. I used to get 'em from the VA, and if I were willing to deal with those bleep-ups, I'm sure I could again. But, you know, I can't go back there, not after everything they did!" He looks away and blushes. I realize that he isn't embarrassed about having to catheterize himself but about the fact that he has taken to using aquarium tubing so he doesn't have to face the VA. And maybe his embarrassment isn't such a bad thing. Maybe putting a dirty, homemade catheter through his urethra and into his bladder is something he needs to rethink.

Mot became estranged from the VA after a surgery to remove a benign tumor from his spine at the base of his skull. I don't know the details, but now that I know that it cost him access to medical supplies he needs daily, I need him to explain it to me.

In his version of the story, a nurse dropped him while he was being transferred from the gurney to a bed after the surgery and he lashed out at her, angry and frightened. "It wasn't me," he says. "I mean, I wasn't the one doing the talking and the threatening, but I could hear it. But what would you do? You've just had major surgery, you have sutures along your spine, and this slob drops you! I mean, wouldn't you be mad?"

"Of course I would!" I say, certain that this can't be the whole story. Surely VA nurses are used to being yelled at, and even threatened, by angry veterans? Veterans have a lot to be angry about.

"They red-flagged you just for that?" I ask.

"No. For that they just gave me a warning. Afterward, they sent me to this halfway house where I was supposed to recuperate, but they couldn't take me because I couldn't walk up and down stairs. Said the VA knew that and shouldn't have sent me. So they just put me out. I mean, here I was, with bandages and stitches and everything but with no place to go. I had a bunch of appointments at the VA I had to keep or risk being paralyzed, so I figured I couldn't just leave town."

I nod, more disturbed by how possible the story sounds than anything. I spent several years working at a Center for Independent Living and know how easily a person can be denied the basic necessities for a minimally decent life simply because he can't walk up a flight of stairs, or requires an attendant to help him bathe, or is unable to navigate the complicated systems that make up our so-called safety net.

"So I figured the best place for me was on the grounds of the VA. I mean, I could barely walk. The VA was a ways outside of town and hard to get to and from. You could call a van to pick you up, but I didn't have a phone or an address, so what was I supposed to do?" Mot looks at me, and I nod. He often checks to be certain that he is being reasonable, particularly when someone else has suggested that he isn't. "So anyway, this guard saw me and told me I had to leave. I tried to explain it to him, but he didn't care. I mean, I knew he was just doing his job, but I don't like being run off, so I refused to go. He calls another guard, and things get a little physical. But really, it took two guards to get me out the gate, and I was pretty beaten up from the surgery. Can you imagine?" He whistles.

"Anyway, they red-flagged me after that. Said if I wanted to come back, I had to call first and arrange to have an armed escort at all times." He throws up his hands in a gesture of defeat. "And, I mean, I wasn't going to do that. That's ridiculous! So I just decided not to have anything else to do with them."

"But what about the catheters? Don't you need them?"

Mot glares at me. "I said, I'm not going to have anything else to do with those bleep-ups, and that's that. Done deal. What are you, some kind of government shill?"

I let it drop, grateful at least for the hint. His illness plays fair most of the time. Before it makes Mot believe a thing about me—that I'm a government shill, or that I want to force his surrender—it usually gives me a warning. I suspect that eventually I will miss one, or one too many, and then delusion will cut the bond between us. But today, I am glad to have the trap pointed out, and I step gingerly around it.

"Okay. But I'm going to go ask for extra catheters again. Maybe I can talk to a different nurse this time. I'll be back in a little bit."

Mot nods and closes his eyes. I stand by the curtain a moment, watching him fall asleep. The long, slender scar that runs from the base of his skull to between his shoulder blades is visible through the open back of the hospital gown. I try to imagine what it would be like to recover from such a dramatic surgery while sleeping on the ground outside a VA hospital in New England during the cold part of spring. I can't. Privilege protects me from understanding that kind of suffering. But I am angrier than I know how to be and keep still.

I ask the nurse for a single catheter and follow her as she retrieves it. She has put a box of catheters of the right size on the floor in the nurse's station. She very pointedly hands me only one. "If he needs another," she says, "have him ring his bell and I'll bring it. No need for you to be prowling around after them." But I am. I walk to the door as if I am headed to the cafeteria, but as soon as she is gone, I am at the box, cramming handful after handful into my purse.

Some things are worth stealing.

CAR TALK

A car can massage organs which no masseur
can reach. It is the one remedy for the disorders
of the great sympathetic nervous system.
—Jean Cocteau

The Saturday after Mot gets out of the hospital, I'm
on *Car Talk*. Mot and I sit in his apartment, listening together as Tom and
Ray consider the question of the summer thermostat.

"Next we have Sarah from Morgantown, W.V.," one of them says. I
have a hard time telling the two men apart; one has a slightly more gravelly
voice and wanders off into funny more often than the other. "Is that Sarah
with an h?"

"It is." They always ask this question. In fact, they pay an odd amount
of attention to the name of the caller. But as they are asking me, I see the
purposefulness in the asking. I'm nervous, but not so nervous I can't remember how to spell my name. It's a trick to put me at ease, and it works.
By the time we're done talking about whether or not I'm a *Sarah-with-an-h*
it feels like just another conversation.

"So, Sarah, tell us what's wrong with your car," asks the one I think is
Tom.

"Well, I have a 1999 Camry, and I took it this summer to Oklahoma to
visit a friend, and as we were driving around the incredibly, ridiculously
hot highways of Oklahoma, he kept insisting that my car was running
too hot even though the temperature gauge showed that it was just about

in the middle or maybe a little above." I say all this in a rush. I have been practicing, afraid I'll get some of the information wrong.

"Yeah, go on . . ." Ray says encouragingly.

"He said the problem was that I didn't have a summer thermostat, and I'd never heard of one, so he took me to a parts store and showed me they existed, because I thought maybe he was making that up. So I drove the car back to West Virginia and asked my mechanic, and he said, 'Oh, summer thermostats are a thing of the past and you don't need one on this car.'" This isn't actually true. My original mechanic had said he'd never heard of a summer thermostat. The mechanic I replaced him with, after Mot showed me a summer thermostat in a Pep Boys, said I didn't need one. But it seemed unnecessarily complex to explain this to the *Car Talk* guys.

"Tell us about this guy," says Tom. I hadn't expected them to ask any questions about Mot himself, and I hesitate a second before answering. I'm not sure what to say. That he's my homeless friend who not only fixes junked cars but lives in them? That he's sitting with me, listening, and I don't know how he'll react if they say something derogatory about him?

"Is this guy between zero and fifty?" asks Ray, breaking my silence.

"No, my friend is in his sixties. And is an expert at picking up old cars and . . ."

"Oh, I thought you were going to say an expert at picking up young girls!" Ray says.

"Maybe that, too!" Tom interjects.

"Well, he's living in the past."

"Oh, he's going to be so brokenhearted that you said that," I reply. I'm watching Mot, who screwed up his face at the comment about picking up young girls, and again when they said he was living in the past. But he seems to know that they talk about everyone like this, and so he smiles and nods when he sees me watching him.

"You can certainly put a lower-temperature thermostat in there, but that's not what it was designed to have. And if it's 120 degrees out, you're going to overheat. All it's going to do is maybe delay it for a few minutes," offers Tom.

"Do you have any idea what it was that gave him this thought?" asks Ray.

"Yes, as we were driving—because he had driven with me in this car in

West Virginia, too—he felt we didn't have the same amount of pickup that we had before, even though the roads were flat there and they're never flat here." Mot shakes his head at me. Clearly I've gotten something wrong in trying to explain his concerns to the Magliozzi brothers, although Mot doesn't say what.

"And he was attributing not having enough pickup with having the wrong thermostat?" asks Ray.

"Sure," Tom interjects. "The engine was running too hot, the pistons were all swelled up and getting stuck in the cylinders and couldn't move up and down as freely as they would if the engine was cooler. . . . It all makes perfect sense." He pauses. "If you're a nut job!"

Now I'm watching Mot closely. I hadn't given any thought at all to the way Tom and Ray throw around words like wacko and nut job and crazy. But Mot seems calm. He's alternately watching me and staring out the open door of his apartment at the hillside, shaking his head.

"How good a friend is this guy?"

"A very good friend," I say, slowly and deliberately. Mot continues shaking his head.

"So you'll have to break it to him gently, then," says Tom.

"So you can't dump him," laughs Ray.

At this, Mot sits up and looks startled for a second.

"No," I say. I try to make eye contact with Mot, but he's now staring straight ahead, listening to the show but paying me no mind.

"No, no. I think you have to tell him that you've talked to us, and your regular mechanic in West Virginia . . ." Tom begins.

". . . and we all think he's wacko!" Ray finishes.

"Yeah," agrees Tom, and they both laugh.

"Gently like that," I say, making my voice light and teasing. Mot hears the laughter in it and relaxes back into the couch.

Tom says, "Yeah, gently like that."

"Uh, Bill," suggests Ray, "they think you're a wacko." They both laugh heartily, and now Mot, remembering that it's a joke, winks at me and whispers, "Maybe my next name will be Bill."

"But no, modern cars have a certain-temperature thermostat in there, usually it's something like 190 degrees," Tom explains, "and it stays there forever. If it ever malfunctions, you replace it with the same kind of thermostat, the same rating. And the reason the temperature is that high is that you want the engine to reach operating temperature as quickly as possible, so the thermostat doesn't open up and permit circulation of the coolant into the radiator until the temperature of the engine coolant is 190 degrees. That's so the engine warms up faster and runs more efficiently and as such runs more cleanly. Once that thermostat is open, and that water is coming out at 190 degrees, if it's a 120-degree day, it's going to be well above that, so having a 180-degree thermostat really isn't going to change anything at all, except to reduce your mileage and reduce your efficiency while the engine is warming up. So it's really a waste."

This is all nonsense to me, but Mot is nodding and picks up a pencil and a piece of a cardboard moving box. He begins to draw an engine, and to trace the flow of coolant through it, while he listens.

"Okay, so definitely not a new thermostat then," I say, because that's the only part of his explanation that I understood.

Ray asks, "What car does your friend drive?"

I shoot Mot a look. I'm afraid that a specific answer, or even an answer suggesting that he is now in Morgantown and not still out west somewhere, could trigger his paranoia. "Right now, I don't think he's driving one at all." Mot doesn't react. This must have been a safe enough thing to say. I wish that they'd stop asking questions about Mot and stick to the car, but of course I listen to the show all the time and should have foreseen this, planned for it. I'm careful about the answers I give. I'm certain that Mot can handle being wrong about the thermostat. I'm not so sure that he's up to hearing himself discussed on national radio, particularly by people who are saying he's nuts, a wacko. "He was driving some sort of giant, ancient American sedan that was around with the stegosaurus."

"Well, that explains it!" Ray says.

"And if the truth be known, older cars often required a change of thermostat with the season. But that went out . . ." Tom says.

"Thirty years ago!" Ray interrupts.

"That went out when my brother was still in high school!"

"And that was a long time ago!"

Mot chuckles at this back-and-forth, the first time he has really laughed since the phone call began.

"Good-bye, Sarah."

My good-bye is lost as the engineer cuts from my call to the next segment. I stand for a second, my hands on my hips, my head cocked, looking questioningly at Mot. Are we going to be okay?

Mot looks back at me and shakes his head. "How could they tell I'm nuts just from that one little question?" he asks. "And how come they didn't think you were nuts? I mean, they went right to me, but they totally skipped over the possibility that you're the one who is wacko."

I laugh. "Well, maybe they thought my wackoness was obvious to their listeners."

"That's probably what it was," Mot agrees with surprising seriousness. "They could probably just tell you're a nut job." He picks up the drawing he's made and studies it for a moment. "No summer thermostat, huh? Not for thirty years. Well, that just goes to show how out of touch I am, I guess," he sighs.

"Are you hungry?" I ask. It's a little past lunchtime.

"Yeah, but I'm cooking today. We're not eating anything but rice and onions and garlic. You're too fat, and I need the onions and garlic to keep my blood pressure down." I don't flinch. He's been called crazy half a dozen times on national radio. It seems only fair that I take a knock or two as well.

When I get home, there's a long message on my answering machine from my father. He rarely calls me because neither one of us likes telephones much. We are email or conversation-over-coffee kinds of people.

"They did a bad job of explaining the summer thermostat to you on *Car Talk* this morning," he says. I'm surprised he had a chance to listen to it. Saturday is one of his busiest days.

"The thing is, you changed your thermostat back when all there was to put in your radiator was water, before we had antifreeze." His explanation is a long cant in the arcane language of engineers, and I don't understand it. I take notes, though, so that tomorrow I can try to tell Mot what he said.

"And they weren't very nice to your friend Mot, either," my father finishes. "I thought they were very presumptuous. It makes perfect sense that a guy in his sixties might suggest you change your thermostat." Dad is also a guy in his sixties, one year younger than Mot. "And Tom and Ray aren't exactly spring chickens!" He laughs. "Good-bye, sweetie. Come home soon. We miss you."

I'm forty-two years old with my own house and family, but everyone in Huntington—my parents, siblings, even old friends—says *come home*, not *come visit*, when inviting me there. As I make dinner, I think about this and about what it would be like to have no home at all. Lucy comes in to peer into the pots. I'm making her favorites: ribs on the grill, macaroni and cheese, and absolutely no vegetables. She gives me a hug.

"Thank you, Lady," she says in the funny, half-accented voice we use to talk with one another.

"You're welcome, Lady," I answer.

"You stink, Lady," she says, grabbing a Sprite and getting down the plates to set the table.

"Only because you just hugged me and got me all stinky, Lady," I answer, and she tosses a wadded napkin at my head.

Mike comes up the basement stairs. "Hey, I heard you on *Car Talk* today. Was Mot bummed out that they said he was wrong?"

"No, but he was a little bummed out about being called old and crazy."

Mike laughs. "I'm heading out to visit friends. Do you need me to walk the dogs or anything?" He is helpful and never leaves without first asking if we need him to walk the dogs, take out the trash, or run an errand. It's clear that he's both grateful for the place in our family and always a little afraid that we are about to yank it away.

"Yeah," Lucy says. "I need you to make the Lady not stink so much."

Mike laughs. "Nothing I can do about that. Sorry, kiddo."

After Mike leaves, I ask Lucy if she minds that he lives with us, or that I spend so much time with Mot. I ask her this all the time because it doesn't seem right to bring these people into her life without her permission.

"No, I like Mike," she says. "I guess when I first met him, it seemed a little strange. But Mike and Mot are both nice. And, I mean, you couldn't kick Mike out now. This is his home, right?"

"Right," I say, thinking, *What an amazing kid.*

"I guess it might seem strange that you went to visit Mot," she says, getting down the glasses and filling them with ice. "But only to somebody who doesn't know you, really." She laughs. "You're a weirdo."

I throw the balled-up napkin back at her. "Call your father for dinner. He's upstairs working in his office."

Scotti comes downstairs and we sit around the table, eating and talking about little things: the movie Lucy is going to see that evening with her friends, whether or not the dogs need a bath. The farther I get from Friendship Room, the easier things are for all of us.

MOT, GONE

The art of losing isn't hard to master;
so many things seem filled with the intent
to be lost that their loss is no disaster.
—**Elizabeth Bishop**

        The apples on our trees are at the point where they must be used or lost. I had promised Mot I would come by early this morning, but instead I pick a basket of apples and make pies. Scotti hovers around the kitchen. It's a rare day when he doesn't have to run off to the office or see Rita first thing. We drink coffee and talk about what needs to be done around the house before winter comes. It's the sort of morning that, when I decided to marry him, I imagined we might have often. I don't think twice about being late for Mot. *Early* is a vague word, and any time before noon is still morning.

        Mot and I are going to campus to watch *Les Maîtres Fous* again, this time in the university's AV room instead of on the screen of his laptop, broken up into ten-minute segments posted on YouTube. Mot has promised to explain the significance of demon possession to the *Hauka*, and I'm hoping his explanation will give me some clue about what the *Big Guys Upstairs* are up to. They've been quiet lately, though clearly they're behind his sudden fascination with Agamemnon's death mask and the Knights Templar.

        He'd been distant and wary since the *Car Talk* interview, but then yesterday it seemed we were close again in the easy, familiar way we'd been during my trip to Amarillo. His sudden return to intimacy—the way he put his hand on my shoulder to turn me toward a tree he wanted me to see, the sly good-bye kiss he placed on my cheek before I drove him home—confuses me, but I see these little gestures as reasons to be hopeful. He'd been cheerful on the phone last night, saying that if he knew what was good for him he'd settle down and build a home on the back of mudslide slim. I'd assumed he meant the hillside on which his apartment sat, uneasily and at an odd angle that left his front stoop awash in mud and branches after every rain. When I left yesterday afternoon, he and the landlord's son had been trying to grade the dirt road that led to the building. It was something they did after every heavy rain, and I was glad it meant there was enough work that Mot would be able to pay off his half of October's rent.

I drive along, half an apple pie on the seat beside me. It's the one treat Mot allows himself. "Pie," he says, "at least homemade pie, is the sort of thing it wouldn't be nice to refuse. So even though I don't think I should eat it, I don't want to hurt your feelings." And then, every time, he eats half a pie in only a few minutes. It's comforting to have him accept something from me and nice to see him enjoy himself.

I haven't told him, but I'm hoping that after the film Mot will go with me to the registrar's office to find out what he needs to do to be admitted to WVU. His stories suggest that he'd been able to stay in Vermont longer than he'd stayed anywhere else, and I assume it was because he enjoyed his classes. He has often mentioned that it's one of the few things he's proud of having done and that he would like to finish his degree. Maybe keeping him busy and engaged in meaningful work will be the secret to keeping him here, at least through the winter.

I park on the hard road and make the muddy climb to Mot's apartment on foot. The dirt road up the hill is more stream than street, and I've lived in West Virginia long enough to know better than to drive it. The tractor Mot and the landlord's son had been using sits halfway up the hill, stranded in a gully. Almost all the gravel they'd laid the day before has washed away.

I know as soon as I walk into the apartment that Mot has packed up and left. The red and black wool blanket and his backpack, shoes, and clothes are gone. Because it's possible, although not likely, that he has taken all these things with him while he washes his clothes, I walk down and check the laundry room. It's empty, and the machines are all still and cool to the touch. No one has done any washing this morning. I go back upstairs and begin opening drawers and cabinets. I'm relieved that he has taken his blood pressure medicine and sorry to see that he has left the computer, the phone, and the camera.

He has left everything in neat piles: most for me, some for the Salvation Army, and one he clearly meant to be left for the next tenant of this lousy apartment. The computer desk he'd made from Sheetrock has been disassembled and the parts hidden in a back closet. He doesn't like to leave behind anything made by his own hands. But he hasn't destroyed the ladder-back chair he reupholstered with damask cloth, and I take it for my writing desk. I leave the second one, which he never got around to fixing, for the next unlucky tenant. I'd like to believe that he left the finished one for me, but it's more likely that he didn't think to tear it apart. The houseplants are neatly lined up near the window. I leave them so that I can't turn caring for them into a false magic.

Even though I've known all along that we were fighting history, I can't help feeling that Mot's going is my fault. It's been like this all along. His own belief in the power of the Others has always left me with the sense of having magic of my own, and I end up interrogating myself for the ways in which I've failed to use powers I never had in the first place.

It will be years before I understand that nothing I could have done would have made a difference, that if the Others could be beaten, Mot would have beaten them years before. And even longer before I believe that even though we failed, trying was still the right thing to have done. We did what we could, and when it was clear that it wasn't enough, he had the grace and the strength to move on. Eventually, I will come to see his moving on as a kindness. But now I feel that I've failed him, and that it's my fault he'll spend another difficult winter living out of doors.

I stand for a while fingering the leaves of the rubber plant he bought only a few days before at Walmart, trying to find the clue I must have missed. In every other instance, the illness gave me a hint when I came close to making a mistake that would break us apart. But no matter how carefully I mull over our last few visits, I can't find any sign that he was planning to leave. Had he known for a while that he would be heading out today, or did he wake up this morning to discover that it was time to go? It will be a long time before I accept that I won't ever know.

I'm out the door and about to drive away before I think to go back and check his hiding place beside the refrigerator. There isn't a note, but he has left the $175 I'd given him toward the next month's rent and a list of the hours he'd worked for the landlord. I wish he'd taken the cash—he'll need it more than I will—but I also know that he left it because he's not a thief, and even if he thought I'd betrayed him, he would not steal from me.

I call the landlord, who is surprised and surly, at least as upset about losing his handyman as about the broken lease. I suspect the landlord's son might know something—he and Mot had been digging a new drainage ditch with a backhoe when I left them yesterday afternoon—but I don't go and knock on his door. Mot would find my doing so an invasion of his privacy. All along, our agreement was that I wouldn't stand in the way of the things he felt compelled to do, even when I didn't understand why he needed to do them. I won't violate that now.

Still, I need to make some effort, to be able to say to myself that I did not give up too easily, so I spend the next hour driving the highways leading out of town, looking for Mot near the on-ramps. There is no Greyhound or Amtrak station in Morgantown, so I can't imagine how he could get out of town without hitchhiking. But he has told me that he doesn't hitch because he can't stand the idea of being stuck in a car with a stranger. Maybe he talked another tenant into giving him a ride to Pittsburgh, where he could catch a bus back west, or maybe he took a local bus to a nearby town. I will never know. The only attempt I make to find him is this aimless driving from exit to exit. I look for him only where I know he won't be found. It's a compromise that Mot would understand.

I don't know why Mot left on this particular day, but as I drive I realize that there were clues. He had taken to telling me that he was meant to be alone, and for the last few days he had been saying, "I can't be where I want to be because I'll only bring death." These weren't startling claims; they didn't sound very different to me from his early warnings that the Big Guys Upstairs didn't want me around and that he wasn't sure he could keep me safe from them. And in spite of these new warnings, we'd had many good days in these last few weeks. We'd driven to the lake, walked by the river, watched the boats and talked about his improbable designs for better ones.

I sift through the past week looking for clues. There was the sly kiss on my cheek as I let him out of the car yesterday, perhaps a kiss good-bye.

And his cryptic reference to "mudslide slim." *If I'm smart, and I am, I'll try to figure a way to create a living environment on the back of mudslide slim.* At home, I ask Scotti if that has any meaning to him, and he immediately recognizes it as the title of a James Taylor album. I buy the CD, but listening to it doesn't shed any light on Mot's reasons for leaving.

WHAT'S LEFT BEHIND

All day I think about it, then at night I say it. Where
did I come from, and what am I supposed to be
doing? I have no idea. My soul is from elsewhere,
I'm sure of that, and I intend to end up there.
—Rumi

In the weeks after Mot leaves, I am forced to face an
unpleasant truth about myself: I'm as relieved that he's gone as I am sorry.
I wanted to be his friend for the long haul, but as his delusions shifted and
his trust in me eroded, the work of trying to keep up with the machina-
tions of the *Big Guys Upstairs* had worn me down. Reorienting him in the
here and now, addressing the litany of accusations against me every morning, was hard work. Within a week of his moving into the apartment on
Breezy Drive, he was uneasy about being there. It was clear that he wasn't
going to be able to settle in permanently and that the best I could hope to
do was help him stay through the cold winter months. But keeping him
here had become difficult, draining work, and there were days when the
time and energy I spent helping him hold on felt like too much to ask of
myself. My sadness at his leaving is tempered by my relief that I no longer
have to try.

I spend my time now doing the things I missed while he was here:
having lunch with friends, reading the stack of books I bought but left
unopened over the months of our friendship, perfecting my recipes for
kimchi and apple pie. I spend more time with Lucy, who has grown into

a young woman I would want as my friend even if she weren't my stepdaughter. We go shopping; I dye her hair a shocking blue that her mother hates and her father pretends not to mind; we watch television and talk about the boy she likes and the boy who likes her and why it seems that in junior high the two are never the same person. I promise her that it gets better and work hard not to let her see the gulf between her father and me, though we both roll our eyes when he leaves the room to spend an hour on the phone with Rita, and though Lucy still sometimes asks why Rita is more important to him than she is. "She isn't," I say, and I mean it. "He just knows you're safe, and she's not." But like Lucy, I'm not satisfied that it's an adequate reason for him to leave us so much alone.

I consider going back to work, but the only agencies that are hiring work with the same people I used to see at Friendship Room, and that's work I can no longer do. I still donate money, help out with fundraisers, and organize donation drives. But I'm done with being on the front lines of the battle against homelessness. I go to graduate school instead, studying writing instead of social work.

My limitations are more obvious to me, and I now know that wanting to do a thing isn't the same as being able to do it. In the first few weeks after Mot's departure, the realization makes me stingy and mean. The generosity that let me open my home to people who needed a place to rest had seemed the best part of me, and I'm not certain how to like this less charitable version of myself.

Mike has taken to staying in the basement while we're awake, sneaking upstairs only after he's sure we've gone to bed and microwaving some awful thing he's spent his food stamps on: a half-dozen Jimmy Dean Griddlecake Sandwiches, a Family Size Stouffer's Meatloaf, Banquet Salisbury Steaks and Brown Gravy. The dogs jump off the bed and scratch at the bedroom door as soon as they hear him in the kitchen, and they whine until the stench of the cheap meat in the frozen meals has faded into a sort of damp, mildewy smell and Mike has gone back downstairs. I lie in bed, listening to the dogs, and wonder when I will finally be able to ask Mike to leave. He has been here a year and a half now, and he isn't any closer to resolving his issues with Social Security than he was when he moved in. He misses appointments, fails to file paperwork, gets frustrated and lets the whole process grind to a halt, and then has to start over. And I am too worn out to take over and do the work for him.

I can't even say, exactly, what it costs us to have him here. Nothing, really. A few minutes' wakefulness in the night, a room in the basement we wouldn't use for anything but storage if he were gone. Even knowing that, the burden of his presence is quickly overtaking the depths of my compassion.

It's one thing never to take responsibility for another person. It's something entirely different to put that responsibility aside once you've taken it up. I want Mike to move out and Scotti to rid himself of his obligations to Rita, but neither of us is able to walk away from the promises we've made, and except for Mot, the people we've promised to help don't seem inclined to walk away from us.

Our marriage is floundering. I can no longer tolerate the way our life together is delineated by other people's emergencies. I tell my friend Kevin that I think it's time for the homeless guy in my basement to move out, and he says, "If he lives in your basement, then he isn't really homeless." And it's true. Mike's only homeless if I want him to be. The burden of that, the way in which the needs of the people we've reached out to outstrip my ability to respond, has become too much for me, and I want to say *enough* and close the circle around our home, locking out everyone but Scotti, Lucy, and myself. But Scotti only knows how to live expansively and—perhaps rightly—thinks his commitment to Rita is too great to let the whims of his wife be the reason he stops being her caretaker.

We make accommodations. I no longer answer the phone because I can't take it when Rita screams at me that if I don't put Scotti on the phone *right now* she is going to run away, or kill herself, or burn down her house. If we run into her at the store or on campus, I try to duck out of sight because it upsets Rita to see Scotti and me together. I have, I know, deserted her, and it's an unkind thing to have done, but it feels strange to be hiding from her, as if I were his mistress and she the one with the rightful claim. There is no room for me at the center of Scotti's life, and I've grown tired of getting by on what little emotional energy he has to give after a day spent tending to her. But I also know that I'm the one who has changed; the situation hasn't. I'm going back on the tacit agreement we made when we married: to be people who do these sorts of things and make these kinds of sacrifices. He's still the man I married, but I'm a different person now. Less generous, more willing to insist on my own place at the table.

Self-sacrifice no longer calls to me. I've given too much of myself away already, and it has done too little good.

The problem of what to do about Mike is solved quickly enough. Early in my first semester of graduate school, a classmate who lives a few houses away tells my pedagogy class that the police knocked on her door at midnight the night before, looking for someone named Michael-something because he'd been involved in an assault. A phone call later I know that it's our Mike. The police tell me that he's wanted for assault but won't give me any details. This terrifies me. I arrive home in a rage, demanding that he leave immediately and saying that if he doesn't turn himself in, I will call the police myself. This is not a person I have ever known myself to be, this woman who screeches and commands. I interrogate myself to see if, as Mike and Scotti both suggest, I am being unreasonable, and I decide that I'm not. That in fact it's very reasonable not to want the police to go knocking on the neighbors' doors looking for someone who is living with us and not to want to have someone living with us who is wanted by the police for assault.

Mike calls, and the police take him off to jail. It turns out that he's wanted for an accident, not an assault, that happened months ago. He had been trying to sell a hunting knife he'd found and had handed it blade-first to a man who was considering buying it, slicing open the man's palm. In the intervening months, the two had a falling-out, and now the man is pressing charges. The police, who have a record of the incident and a statement from the victim that the stabbing was indeed accidental, call to tell me that the charges will be dropped. I'm not mollified. It may not be a crime, but there was still a knife, and the police were still knocking on the neighbors' doors. It takes the system several days to sort things out, and Mike spends them at Doddridge County Jail. By the time he's out, we all know that I won't let him move back into the house. He packs his belongings and returns to the homeless shelter. Nothing is different for him than it was before we took him in. He's no closer to getting his disability benefits, a job, or an education. When he leaves, we all promise to keep in touch. Of course, we don't.

For six months, I've been sending Mot an email every Monday. Simple things. In April, I send one that reads:

I think I remember that April is your birth month, though I don't
remember the day. So, happy Birth Month! I will save you the singing,
which I do badly, but wish you were here so that I could buy you the
traditional steak dinner. I hope all is well.

And for the first time since he left, I get a response:

Although I do run across things that cause a . . . does Sarah know
about blah, blah.
None the less I do have an onboard prog that differs from the unme
you seem to press for. Allow me:

A certain Patriarch cruises over with a tail longer than he desires,
seeking info (about your buddy jah jah—u remember the one, ('I'll
distract him, u come up from behind & bleep him') concerning jah
jah's possibility of reentering the scene as a player. After killing all of
those Jews in W II it isn't in his best interest.

This causes me to think; you are a mock jewess at best. Of course we
both heard the closing; 'He swallows'. The question I pose to you is;
of whom did he speak. Considering your vain stupidity—It was all for
you. Right? Not.

2. You seem to continue to be driven into dementia because of 'The
Purse Strings of Crypt Manor'. Sure you'll get a little something, but
never control. The puppet master isn't stupid. You know you'll still play
a part, I not doubting that.

3. The grey bad hair day person would like to twist your neck off to
replace it with a proper one I would hope. Put the current one on a
ranging beast I would think.

4. How dare you endorse Holocaust Remembrance when you're
dancing with the who dunnit.

More, I can think of, but this is making me sick. Don't reply. Don't call
me, I won't call u.

You know the condition over here, better than any one ever—and look
what you did you insecure (bleepch) play Spike the Kyke 27 times in a
row. I needed someone.

There is no signature. He isn't Mot, or Tom, S/mot. I'm not sure who he is, and I can't follow the stream of delusion. Momentarily heartened by the opening line, I write back, admitting that I may have been tricked into doing something awful but never intended it and don't even know what it was, reminding him that I am on his side, that I cast a shadow. And for a moment, it seems as if these old tactics may work. He answers me the next day.

> sorry about the mock. I didn't feel good about writing it . . .

> Look (but you don't question), it's taken me many years to crawl around trying to find my niche. 6th grade I told my best friend (3 previous friends, that I loved even more, had already moved away). You'll pull ahead of me Johnnie, I'm being left out. I knew inherently. Little things along the way. Why go into this, it's been explained, you choose not to believe. Why, indeed would such a high flying mind as ja's single me out.

> Sure he's gone through the rigamarole over here. 1. Getting me to try kill me self (just returned from Erin—even on the radio it's me this me that). No results. 2. Now watch as the man turns into a woman—tah dah. I said now watch . . . (nada) 3. He knew his brother was headed here so why not him. Saw what bro was attempting with the dolphin machine (trying to attach an old whore to me). Hee hee, I played a joke. I said, 'Oh no she's here'. In a flash ja was down to stick in her and in an instant they both toppled into her coffin (you had to have been there).

He played the German card:

> 'I can prove absolutely, beyond a shadow of a doubt this individual having already been troubled by the law, did terminate a union with a wonderful *machen* he, without a doubt abused. Adding further worry and deep concern to her parents, both of whom supported him. This gratitude and support thrown asunder by this low class brut' (Something to that effect—you know how he likes to use the law). The frau was brought forward. What's wrong? I was shining as the star. The Parents were brought. Bong. I loved them both, they faded.

'Okay let's look at the dutch friends'. again no problem except for Fritz, he called me out when we were passing class in the hall (hi sch). I was scared, but I showed. Fritzie jumped into Larry's flat head and they sped away. I got one kick in, rear passenger door, driver's side.

Then it went off into the repetitive. Polish Pickle, Polish pickle, Polish Pickle, Polish pickle, Polish Pickle, Polish pickle, Polish Pickle, Polish pickle, Polish Pickle, Polish pickle, Polish Pickle, Polish pickle, Polish Pickle, Polish pickle, (others were listening in—H. Ford said "The old guy (the one we love to hear) is finally losing it." Eventually, after a bunch more of Polish Pickle, Polish pickles, a scene evoked on a football field, a pro coach I admired, had a barrel of P.p's on the side line. He reached in, savoring one looking up at me. I said: "Hey! Could I have one?" (not the desired response)

I guess not the desired effect.

Yes much more to tell. But I've already told. Yet I know there is much I don't know. I told you I didn't need much, that there were some here that would resist. Remember, so much time invested in me they wouldn't let me go. I need help in understanding, they don't want me do and now you don't

but i gotta go now times hour is kicking in

This makes no more sense to me than it would make to a stranger. I can't parse any of it or find meaningful fragments of the old narrative. I try telling him I can't understand, asking for his help, and he writes one more time, but the email is completely incoherent. It's exactly like the word salad he spit out when I asked him why his sister wouldn't speak to him in Amarillo: he forgets to use verbs; affirmative statements become negative ones midsentence; only half a word gets said before he's on to the next. I can't tell if he's trying to explain, telling me to leave him alone, or both. When I try to write back, I find that he has closed his email account. I get only a message from the servers at Yahoo telling me that no such address exists. And with that, the last tie between us is severed. I have no way to reach him, and I suspect that he hasn't taken my email address with him so that he would have a way to reach me. The *Others* wouldn't allow it.

There is no mistaking that he's beyond me now. I'm sad to have lost him, but I'm also relieved that he hasn't asked the impossible of me: that I be the person I had once promised I would be, one who believed that his illness was manageable and that friendship might be enough to overcome it. That person is gone. In her place, there is only a middle-aged woman who knows her own limitations well and has come to accept that some things can't be changed.

I wish for him another blind optimist who doesn't know this yet, and another, and another after that, enough that there will always be someone who worries about him when it's too cold to be sleeping out of doors, who listens to his stories about Albania and Italy, who buys him dinner on his birthday. For myself, I wish only for a quieter life. I read his email one last time and then turn off the computer and walk into the kitchen to wash the breakfast dishes and make a cup of tea.

It's a beautiful spring morning, and I take my mug and my book into the garden, sitting in an old chaise lounge still dirty from winter under the apple trees Mot taught me to prune. They're heavy with flowers; it will be a good harvest come the end of summer. The daffodils bloom around the old chicken coop filled with broken lawnmowers and the cast-off swimming pools and sandboxes of Lucy's childhood, and a mourning dove coos from a nest in its eaves. Red squirrels scamper in the limbs of the old chestnut on the side of the house, and I can smell the freshly turned earth where Scotti has dug a garden for me. Flats of sprouts—Amish Paste and Cherokee Purple tomatoes, ground cherries, cucumbers, and eggplant—sit under protective glass on the porch.

Scotti is at breakfast with Rita, a ritual that begins—but by no means ends—his time with her each day. Lucy is asleep upstairs. She has started sleeping teenage summer hours and rarely wakes up before noon. Only the dogs and I are ever here and awake to enjoy the quiet of these cool mornings. They lie in spots of sun on the grass chasing dream rabbits, old creatures that would rather sleep than play.

I'm trying to learn to be comfortable, to fix the problems I hid from myself while Mot and Mike were here. I work harder at being a wife. I make elaborate pastas every night: rigatoni with sausage and broccoli rabe, manicotti stuffed with spinach and feta in a lemon sauce, angel-hair pasta with capers and crisped prosciutto. I sort the laundry the way Scotti wants: socks and underwear never mixed with shirts, thin cotton separated from denim, towels cleaned every day. I wake up at six to walk the dogs so he can sleep, and I've stopped asking when he's going to clean out the room Mike left empty and turn it into the study he promised me. I've come to understand that these are among the things I can't change, and I am trying to see if I can instead learn to live with them. I have the same urge for going that I felt in Mot after the first days in the apartment on Breezy Drive. Like him, I have a hard time living with rules that aren't my own. Like him, I'm beginning to believe that things might be better elsewhere. Like him, I know that it may only be myself I'm trying to outrun.

EPILOGUE

I've just finished baking Lucy's birthday cake. She'll be twenty-one in a few days, and she and her girlfriend are coming over this evening to celebrate. I'm no longer married to her father, but she is still very much my stepdaughter. She and Kayla now live in the old yellow farmhouse. Scotti lives with his lover and their many dogs out in the country. I live in Athens, Ohio, where I am working toward my PhD in creative nonfiction. We are each happier than we were when we lived together.

Rita's regime of psychotropic medications grew too toxic for her system, and she died in October of 2010 after a series of strokes. Scotti and I were in the midst of finalizing our divorce. At her memorial service, I praised the dedication he had shown to her, and for the first time in a long time, I did so without being bitter about the cost of it.

"Before I met Rita," I said, "I believed that there was dignity in suffering. She taught me that I was wrong. There is no dignity in suffering. The dignity is in rising above your pain and finding a path to joy." And this is true, though of course I didn't say that my learning this meant leaving Rita, and Scotti, behind. Friends pulled me aside to ask if Scotti and I were considering getting back together now that Rita was gone. When I said that we weren't, they almost universally looked relieved. The last years of our marriage were unhappy enough that nobody, my friends or his, ever suggested that we were making a mistake by moving on with our separate lives. Not even Lucy, who loves us both.

In hindsight, I see that we married for the wrong reasons. We should have started a nonprofit organization instead. We shared a cause and mistook it for being able to share a life. I still admire Scotti's work and his willingness to make sacrifices for it. His research into PTSD was and is important, particularly as so many of our troops have returned from wars in Iraq and Afghanistan. What he does matters. I simply wasn't able, in the long run, to do it with him.

According to the Social Security death index, Mot died in October 2011. I know nothing about how he lived in the years after he left Morgantown, and I don't know anything about the circumstances of his death. But I do know that the apartment on Breezy Drive was listed as his last known address, and this makes me unexpectedly sad. I had hoped for him a string of naive, well meaning people who didn't yet know—as I had not yet known—that friendship alone can't fix the violence that our broken system does to people who can't live within it. I had imagined for him a better ending than the one he got.

I think I know now what went wrong. In the beginning, I understood that to Mot the value of our friendship wasn't that I might change his life but that I could accept it as it was. That I could like him, and even see the brilliance in the ways he found to survive, without asking him to change in ways he couldn't.

Together we made the decisions that changed the nature of our friendship. He chose not to stop in any of the many towns along the twelve hundred miles of highway between Oklahoma City and Morgantown, and he chose to accept my offer to help him try living in an apartment for the first time in years. For a while after he left, I forgot those facts. I believed that things fell apart between us because of choices I alone had made. This is the danger of having come to see myself as someone who was helping him rather than as someone who was his friend. I lost sight of the fact that he had his own life to lead, and that the decisions he made about how to lead it were his own to make. When I remembered this, I stopped believing that we had failed and was simply glad that we had tried. There is meaning in attempting difficult things, whether or not you succeed.

My time working with the homeless is over. Like many people who take on this challenging work, the stressors of the job robbed me of my ability to do it effectively. Still, my commitment remains the same. Nowadays, I focus on policy change and education, not because they're more important than direct service but because I'm good at those things. If you have read this story and come away believing that I've absolved you of any need to try to make things better for those living marginal lives, you've misunderstood me. It's shameful that our veterans return from service with serious physical and mental disabilities and that instead of treatment, we give them cots in homeless shelters. That we talk about people "falling through the cracks in the safety net" when in fact we've been dismantling that net since the Reagan years. That most of us can pass a panhandler and believe that we're doing the right thing by not giving him our spare change because we "know" he'll just spend it on alcohol or drugs. We don't know for sure unless we know him and his story, but few of us take that much of an interest. It's easier to believe that people live on the streets because of their moral failings than to admit that it's because of our own.

According to the 2009 Annual Homeless Assessment Report to Congress, nearly 1.56 million people used emergency shelter or transitional housing programs between October 1, 2008, and September 30, 2009. Of these, a third were homeless as members of families including children. More than two-thirds of homeless adults were persons with disabilities. A disproportionate number of homeless teens—between 20 and 40 percent—are members of the LGBTQ community. Many children move directly from foster care to homeless shelters when they age out of the system at eighteen.

I don't pretend to know what it will take to end—or, more realistically, reduce—homelessness. I do know that we've largely stopped trying, claiming to suffer from "compassion fatigue," as if the fact that the poor have grown tiresome is reason enough to ignore them. Cities including Las Vegas, Orlando, Houston, Dallas, and most recently Philadelphia have made it illegal for charitable organizations to provide food to people in the public places where the homeless often congregate. There were 113 attacks on homeless persons in 2010, 24 of them lethal. Nearly half of the offenders were under twenty years old, and the most common motivation for these attacks was thrill-seeking. Only a few cities and states include homelessness in the list of aggravating factors that determine a hate crime.

We can't end homelessness. We can reduce it by providing more affordable housing and support services for those who struggle with physical or mental disabilities that make it difficult for them to maintain their own homes without assistance. But there will always be folk like Mot who simply can't live in traditional housing, and we need to find a way to create communities that can be inclusive of them. Criminalizing poverty and disability won't make either one go away.

If you want to get involved in the struggle to reduce homelessness and to improve the lives of the chronically homeless, the best place to begin is in your own community. You can find opportunities through your local United Way, homeless shelters, and many local churches. It does make a difference when people volunteer their time to serve meals, provide blankets and warm clothing in the winter, and pass out water bottles during the hot months of summer. It has become fashionable to believe that one person can't make a difference, but it isn't true. You can.

To become better informed about policy issues, consider joining the National Coalition for the Homeless or your local Homeless Coalition. All states, most cities, and many towns have advocacy organizations that work directly to help shape local policies and services, and they are always in need of volunteers.